A Christmas Celebration in Song and Story

A CHRISTMAS CELEBRATION IN SONG AND STORY

EDITED BY

Al Remson

A PERIGEE BOOK

A Perigee Book
Published by The Berkley Publishing Group
A division of Penguin Putnam Inc.
375 Hudson Street
New York, New York 10014

Scripture quotations are taken from the
King James Version of the Bible.

First edition: November 1999

Published simultaneously in Canada.

The Penguin Putnam Inc. World Wide Web site address is
http://www.penguinputnam.com

Library of Congress Cataloging-in-Publication Data

A Christmas celebration in song and story / [edited] by Al Remson.
    p.   cm.
    A collection of Christmas songs, poems, and stories with
background information on their history.
    ISBN 0-399-52552-1
    1. Christmas   Literary   collections.   2. Christmas   in
literature.
    I. Remson, Al.
    PN6071.C6C5118   1999
    808.8'0334—dc21   99-39290
                                       CIP

Printed in the United States of America

10 9 8 7 6 5 4 3 2 1

Contents

THE VISIT OF THE MAGI

51

THE MESSAGE OF CHRISTMAS

63

DECEMBER PAGAN FESTIVALS

71

THE STORIES BEHIND THE CHRISTMAS TALES

91

FOREWORD

Sharing Christmas with Al Remson meant sharing in the simplest and most powerful message of all—love. Those of us who were lucky enough to be there with him shared that message with a special warmth and an uncommon intimacy. Al was a unique man who brought his own brand of magic to every Christmas . . . sometimes extravagant, often unexpected . . . but always from the heart.

Al's first book, *Where Did Christmas Come From?*, was just one way of sharing his love for the holiday. As with any new interest, he immersed himself in the topic. There was a wide-eyed wonder that possessed him as he discovered little-known facts. His latest book, *A Christmas Celebration in Song and Story*, combines his love for Christmas with his other lifelong passion—music. Al was proud of these books. The love of learning that made him a successful researcher, academian and psychologist carried over to his pastimes with the same enthusiasm and drive he gave to his work. But no matter how proud he may have been of his many accomplishments, he would be sure to tell you that his greatest accomplishment was reaching a complete understanding of the love he was capable of for his family and friends—not just at Christmas but on every day of the year.

This book is dedicated to that piece of him in all of us.

INTRODUCTION

PAGAN CAROLS AND
RELIGIOUS HYMNS

What is a carol?

What we think of as our favorite Christmas carols are actually a grab bag of old hymns, folk songs, medieval plainsongs, and songs written for other holidays, as well as what are considered to be true, written-for-the-occasion Christmas carols. Today we associate carols with Christmas, but originally carols were not exclusive to the December holiday. There were Easter carols, spring carols, and carols written for many other festive occasions. For over a thousand years, Christmas wasn't thought of as a particularly important religious holiday; the most important church holidays were Easter, Pentecost, and Epiphany.

Though the Nativity celebration may have been a less-than-major religious occasion, there were other, very important festivities in late December. December 25 and the weeks surrounding it were pagan holidays celebrating the winter solstice and the return of the sunlight from the dark days of mid-December. Such celebrations could be found in the British Isles as well as among Germanic and Norse tribes. Later, when the Romans conquered Britain they brought with them their late-December Saturnalia party, honoring Saturn with wild festivities. Tenth- and eleventh-century Viking invaders brought their Yule traditions to the British Isles. In older carols we may still detect influences from these Norse tribes that invaded or settled in Britain. Their lyrics refer to merrymaking and partying and have little religious content. "Deck the Halls with Boughs of Holly" and "Here We Come a-Wassailing" reflect this nonreligious tradition; neither contains direct references to a Christian holiday. The *Merry* in "Merry Christmas" is our Celtic, Germanic, Norse, and Roman legacy by way of the English.

At first, in an effort to win converts, the Roman church permitted the continuation of pagan rituals within the church, as long as their intent was to honor Jesus. In 601, Pope Gregory I gave permission to decorate churches in the same way pagan temples were decorated and to hold Christmas feasts. He added that churchmen could allow animal sacrifices in the church but should "not let them sacrifice animals to the Devil, but to the praise of God . . . and to give thanks to the Giver for all their abundance." As the Christmas Nativity celebration took on added religious importance, Rome's tolerance of pagan practices came under increased criticism from Eastern Christian officials. Rome tried to get rid of non-Christian influences and dedicate the Nativity day to penitence. These more solemn church attitudes are mirrored in old Latin hymns such as "O Come, O Come Emmanuel" and "Adeste Fideles." But what went on in people's homes is probably reflected in the carol "The Twelve Days of Christmas." It describes the courses served at a Christmas feast (turtledoves, French hens, geese) and the entertainment and guests at the party (pipers piping, ladies dancing, lords a-leaping).

THE ORIGIN OF THE WORD
CAROL AND ITS TWO TRADITIONS

And so there are at least two historic Christmastime traditions, one a fun-filled celebration and the other a more solemn religious holiday. Often there were clashes between the two ways of celebrating. These clashes are mirrored in the dispute over what the word *carol* means. There are scholars who believe that the word *carol* comes from the Greek *chori-*, referring to psalms sung in solemn church processionals. As the priests moved forward they sang the following first two lines:

Tidings true there be come new
Blessed be Jesu

The procession stopped, and standing in place, they sang the *stanza* (derived from the same root word as *standing*) of four lines, often in a rhythmic pattern different from that of the first two lines:

Tidings true told there is true;
Jesu to be born of a maid.
Now is fulfilled that prophecy said,
Blessed be Jesu.

The priests moved forward again, repeating the original two-line phrase. Then they stopped again and sang a new four-line stanza. That two-four-two-four processional pattern is what some believe to be the origin of a true carol. Those who believe that "true" carols originated within the church cite "*Veni Redemptor Gentium*" ("Savior of the Nations, Come"), written by St. Ambrose late in the fourth century, as the first carol that celebrates Jesus' coming.

Other scholars believe that carols originated within folk music. They think the word *carol* is derived from the Greek *khoraules*, which referred to a piper who accompanied dancing. During medieval times, when only Latin hymns were permitted inside the church, people gathered in taverns and fields to dance and chant to the music. Over time, these jaunty songs, accompanied by words in the everyday language of peasants and townspeople, came to be called carols. For those who believe that dancing was the original source, carols are sprightly, lively tunes with ordinary words set in almost conversational phrases.

Probably both sources have made a contribution. The two-four-two-four pattern describes only a few of what we think of today as our favorite Christmas carols. On the other hand, the definition of lively dance music, sung in ordinary language, hardly fits "Adeste Fideles" or "Silent Night." For our purposes, let us think of carols as songs usually sung at Christmastime.

THE FAMILY CHRISTMAS CAROL

The conflict between a solemn religious Christmas and a lively holiday filled with merrymaking attracted the attention of St. Francis of Assisi. He wanted to resolve differences between the austerity of the Latin Christmas mass and the behavior of the partygoers. St. Francis thought that the true meaning of Christ's coming lay in its humanity, rather than its divinity. In 1224 he originated the living Nativity scene to tell the miraculous

Christmas story in a way familiar to all—a family and their love for a child. But instead of getting the two sides to meet on common ground, St. Francis began a third tradition—the family Christmas.

The celebration of Christmas as a family holiday spread through the influence of the Franciscans and the aid they got from an unusual carol writer. Four years after St. Francis's death, Jacopone da Todi was born. He became a wealthy lawyer and seemed to have little interest in religion. But when he was twenty-eight, his beloved wife died, and when she was laid out for burial, he discovered that underneath her dress she always wore a hair shirt—a symbol of her religious penitence. Da Todi was deeply moved. Over time he renounced a life devoted to pleasure, gave up his worldly goods and committed himself to furthering the work of the church. He wandered throughout Italy, begging beside the roads, while writing and singing of the need for humility, religious piety, and the humanity of the Christ child. One of his characteristic verses reads:

> *Sweep hearth and floor,*
> *Be all your vessel's store*
> *Shining and clean.*
> *Then bring the little guest*
> *And give Him of your best*
> *Of meat and drink. Yet more*
> *Ye owe than meat.*
> *One gift at your King's feet*
> *Lay now. I mean*
> *A heart full to the brim*
> *Of love, and all for Him*
> *And from all envy clean.*

How different these words are from the two-four hymns! Where St. Ambrose wrote in Latin of fulfilled prophecies, blessings, and tidings, da Todi wrote in everyday language of sweeping the floor, meat and drink, and a heart full of love. Their music was equally dissimilar. Da Todi's work was set to a lively, joyous, popular rhythm, while St. Ambrose's work is thought to have been set to a processional hymn.

The teachings of St. Francis extolled a life of simple piety. Franciscan friars found expression of their views in da Todi's works. They sang his lively carols throughout Italy and brought their music to Germany and France, as well. Though other priestly orders labeled references to food, drink, and familial love as irreverent, the farmers and townsfolk were deeply touched. They called da Todi "the lord's minstrel" and his carols became famous, translated into the everyday languages of many countries.

So, for the last 750 years Christmas carols have reflected three different traditions. The oldest tradition is the pagan tradition of a holiday celebration with feasting, drinking, and a great deal of merriment. The second oldest is the religious tradition of a sacred remembrance of Jesus' birth. It is a heritage both solemn and exultant. The third tradition celebrates Jesus as a child within a family and is echoed in our own emphasis on children and the family setting. Since the time of St. Francis, the traditions have mixed and mingled in a variety of ways within different cultures. In more modern times, those who wrote Christmas carols were often unaware that they were writing out of one tradition or another. Frequently they may have drawn upon two or even all three of these traditions.

To say people "wrote" carols may be misleading. Many of the carols were originally written as poems. Over time, someone would set the poem to a popular melody or Latin hymn. Some words were wed to different pieces of music. Only in the 1800s is it proper to speak of people regularly writing entire carols, music and words, each intended for the other.

Many, though not all, of our favorite carols come to us with an English heritage. Over the years, England underwent a number of religious transformations that left their mark on the carols. Of those that did not originate in England, their translation by the English made them more acessible to the public in the United States.

THE DECLINE OF CAROL SINGING

When the Church of England broke away from the church of Rome, England became fertile ground for various Protestant sects. At the same time, those who favored a return to the authority of the Roman Pope kept attempting to gain power. Both groups grew more extreme in their advocacy. The seventeenth century saw the rise of fundamentalist Puritanism in England. The Puritans preferred hymns and songs that gave instruction in their very strict sectarian doctrines—and one of the Puritan tenets was that the celebration of Christmas was a vestige of the Roman church mixed with the veneration of St. Nicholas.

So when they achieved political power, the Puritans outlawed Christmas. Anyone found celebrating the day was punished with a fine. In a tract written in 1656, the Puritan Hezekiah Woodward calls Christmas Day:

The old Heathen's Feasting Day, in honor to Saturn their Idol-God, the Papist's Massing Day, the Profane Man's Ranting Day, the Superstitious Man's Idol Day, the Multitude's Idle Day, Satan's—that Adversary's—Working Day, the rue Christian Man's Fasting Day . . . We are persuaded, no one thing more hindereth the Gospel work all the year long, than doth the observation of that Idol Day once in a year, having so many days of cursed observation with it.

At this time, carol singing remained popular in Germany and other countries on the continent, but in Puritan-influenced England, carol singing declined and the carols were all but forgotten.

A REBORN TRADITION OF CAROLING

Although caroling can trace a lineage back to wassailers and waits of earlier times, the carolers we think of—in top hats and scarves, muffs and mittens—are Victorians through and through.

The nineteenth century witnessed renewed interest in celebrating Christmas among the English, as well as among their American cousins across the Atlantic. Washington Irving's humorous bestseller *Diedrich Knickerbocker's History of New York* reintroduced St. Nicholas as a popular hero. A few years later Clement Moore's wonderful poem ''A Visit from St. Nicholas'' ('' 'Twas the night before Christmas, and all through the house . . .'') brought Santa Claus and gift giving to much greater popularity. Charles Dickens's *A Christmas Carol* brought the homespun emotional impact of Christmas to an ever-wider audience.

Given this renewed interest in Christmas, Gilbert Davies published *Some Ancient Christmas Carols* (1823) and William Sandys published *Christmas Carols, Ancient and Modern* (1833). Each man thought he was preserving an art form that was likely to disappear in the near future.

In 1840, Queen Victoria married Prince Albert of Germany, and the popular royal couple brought many German influences to England. He introduced England to the Christmas tree, a prominent feature of German celebrations. The tree was a holdover from pagan traditions among Germanic tribes. The carol ''O Christmas Tree'' comes from Albert's influence as well as America's German immigrants. German celebrations had always favored a child-centered, family-oriented Christmas over an austere, latinized celebration. *Away in a Manger* reflects their attitudes, and comes to us filtered through English influences.

The royal couple's Christmas celebrations generated a lot of publicity. Victorian merchants took advantage of renewed public interest and began to promote Christmas cards, Christmas dinner, and the giving of presents. Davies's and Sandys's books of carols went along for the sleigh ride and helped revive interest in carol singing. The growth of choral groups in England and the United States led to the composition of many new carols, and the late nineteenth century saw the birth of many of our current favorites, including "O Little Town of Bethlehem," "Silent Night," and "It Came Upon a Midnight Clear."

In America caroling came back with a vengeance in the 1920s. The National Bureau for the Advancement of Music conducted a poll in 1918 and found that only thirty U.S. cities fostered community carol singing for Christmas. When the survey was repeated in 1928, two thousand cities reported the presence of community carol singing.

Of course, these figures do not reflect the existence of private carolers. Groups who decided to serenade their neighbors or raise money for Christmas charities have frequented the streets on Christmas Eve for many years. They are a familiar sight in many American communities. But no matter where carols are sung across the land, there are a certain few carols that are almost sure to be heard. It is striking that they are a diverse selection, with no one type of carol predominant.

The diversity of emotions expressed in our favorite carols reflects the three traditions—merrymaking, religious, and family oriented—from which Christmas has come. We sing carols of joy and carols that are much more reverent. We sing lullabies to the Christ child and drinking songs with our friends. All of these emotions have become a part of the outpouring of love and goodwill that mark our Christmas celebrations. Behind each of these carols is a fascinating and often adventure-filled story of how it came to be written.

THE TIME OF ADVENT

Advent begins four Sundays before Christmas and ends on Christmas Eve. The period is a celebration of the original coming of Jesus and also a reminder of His second coming in the days ahead.

When the church decided to celebrate the Nativity in the fourth century, it was faced with the fact that there was no record of when Jesus was born—neither the year nor the day and date. December 25 was chosen because it would serve to create a Christian holiday at a time when many pagan holidays were celebrated. Almost all peoples had a holiday associated with the end of the period when the daylight grew less and the sun began to shine for longer periods. For Romans, December 25 was the celebration of *Natalis Solis Invicti*—''The Birthday of the Unconquerable Sun.'' It honored the Persian sun god Mithra; Roman soldiers began to worship Mithra while stationed in the old Persian empire, and the holiday had been popular for more than two hundred years. December was also the time of two other major Roman holidays: Kalends and Saturnalia. For the Norse peoples it was the time of the Yule celebrations. Church leaders felt that if pagan holidays marked the return of the sun, why not set Jesus' birth in December to signify that He is the light of the world?

But while Jesus' Nativity was but a single day, the pagan holidays spread over many weeks. The lone day of Christmas was swamped by the weeks of celebrating that led up to it, filled with food and drink, revels, and debauchery. The Christian church needed to focus its followers on the spiritual message of Jesus' coming and the promise of His return.

And so the church created Advent—originally a forty-day period leading up to Christmas. Their first inclination was to celebrate it the way Lent was observed. As a direct antidote to the temptations of Kalends and Yuletide, the church fathers created a period of fasting and prayer, leading up to midnight mass on Christmas Eve. However, the joyous holiday spirit of December was too strong to sustain a long, somber holiday, and the seriousness of the Advent period began to diminish in people's minds. By the ninth century, Advent had been shortened to four weeks.

The Roman Catholic church continues to honor its original intent for Advent by omitting the traditional joyous hymns ''*Te Deum*'' and ''*Gloria*'' from their services during the month. But this symbolism is apparently lost on most worshipers, who continue to regard the period as a joyous one.

A number of other Advent practices have survived through the centuries. The Advent wreath, a circle of holly or fir boughs, remains popular. The circle symbolizes the perfection and unity of God. The evergreens symbolize His eternal presence and the life force He represents.

Frequently the evergreen wreath serves as a base for candles. A new candle is added on each of the four Sundays of Advent. The first candle is referred to as the Prophecy Candle, signifying the prophecy that the Messiah was coming. As such, it also stands for both the long years of waiting until He did come and the long years that stretch before us until the second coming.

The candle lit on the second Sunday of Advent is called the Bethlehem Candle. It was prophesied in the fifth chapter of Micah that the Messiah would be born in Bethlehem. Micah predicted the destruction of the southern kingdom of Israel by the Assyrians. But he also predicted a time when the Messiah would come, and men

> shall beat their swords into plowshares, and their spears into pruninghooks: nation shall not lift up a sword against nation, neither shall they learn war any more.
>
> (Micah 4:3)

Micah may have been the first person in the Western world to promulgate the ideal of universal peace.

On the third Sunday of Advent the Shepherds Candle is lit. It was to the Galilean shepherds ''keeping watch over their flock by night'' that the angel appeared and said,

Fear not; for, behold, I bring you good tidings of great joy, which shall be to all people.

For unto you is born this day in the city of David a Saviour, which is Christ the Lord.

(Luke 2:10–11)

And the shepherds went to Bethlehem to see for themselves and then spread the word to others. This third candle is to remind everyone to share their knowledge and their spiritual revelations.

The fourth Sunday of Advent is occasion for lighting the final candle, the Angels Candle, to remind us of the angels' Annunciation to Mary and later to the shepherds, and of their presence at the Nativity.

Another widespread Advent tradition comes down to us as the Advent Calendar. It appears to be a direct descendant of what was originally known as an *Advent house*, with windows that opened—one each day—to reveal a scriptural reminder of religious faith. The origins of the house and calendar are not known, but they served to remind the faithful of the month-long religious obligations leading up to Christmas Eve midnight mass.

There is an even older tradition about the four weeks of Advent. Each week was supposed to represent one of the four comings of Christ—the first, His coming as a man; the second, His coming in the human heart; the third, His coming at the death of the worshiper; and the fourth, His second coming on Judgment Day.

In the centuries when most families worked the fields, Advent fell after the harvest and after the thinning of the herds, leaving time to observe the weeks leading up to the Christmas holiday. While an industrialized world cannot afford weeks of religious observance and Advent has diminished in importance, its message of salvation and peace through the coming of the Lord has grown in relevance and significance.

CAROLS

O Come, O Come, Emmanuel

"OCome, O Come, Emmanuel" is an Advent carol, more suitable to the pre-Christmas period that anticipates the coming of the Messiah. The carol has nothing directly to do with the actual birth of Jesus or its celebration.

The coming of a Messiah had been foretold for hundreds of years. References to His coming occur in many books of the Old Testament.

In twelfth-century monasteries, the week preceding Christmas was given over to evening vespers to proclaim the Advent of His coming. For each of the seven nights before Christmas, as the monastic processional moved forward, they invoked His coming with a different name each night: Wisdom, Lord, Rod of Jesse, Key of David, Orient, King, Emmanuel. Because each line of the chant began with "O," as in "O Wisdom" or "O Key of David," the hymn was referred to as "The Great O's," or "The Seven O's."

As torches lit the scene, the priests' processional moved forward through the early evening darkness, and they began the chant with two lines:

Rejoice! Rejoice! Emmanuel
Shall come to thee, O Israel.

Then, the procession would halt and in one voice they would chant the stanza:

O come, O come, Emmanuel,
And ransom captive Israel,
That mourns in lonely exile here
Until the Son of God appear.

By 1851, the tradition of the seven evening processionals was no longer practiced, but the chant remained. John Neale, the man who wrote "Good King Wenceslas," published a *Medieval Hymnal* and provided the translation we now use—but he cut the number of verses from seven to five. The hymnal included the words, but no music.

Three years later, aware that the verses dated back to medieval times, an associate of Neale's, Thomas Helmore, wanted to find a suitable medieval melody. He adapted the melody we know today from twelfth-century plainsongs. Unlike popular songs of today, plainsongs have no measures to indicate their timing. They are chanted in a variety of rhythms and meters, the rhythm often changing line by line to suit the meaning of the words.

Helmore chose well. "O Come, O Come, Emmanuel" echoes the sound of ancient chants and a timeless yearning that reflects humanity's desire for reassurance that God will look after them.

O Come, O Come, Emmanuel

Moderately

1. O come, O come, Im - man - u - el, And
2. O come, O come, Thou Lord _____ of might, Who
3. O come, Thou Rod of Jes - se, free, Thine
4. O come, Thou Key of Da - vid, come, And
5. O come, Thou Day - Spring, come _____ and cheer Our

ran - som cap - tive Is - ra - el That mourns in lone - ly
to Thy tribes, on Si - nai's height, In an - cient times did'st
own from Sa - tan's tyr - an - ny; From depths of hell thy
o - pen wide our heav'n - ly home; Make safe the way that
Spir - it's by Thine ad - vent here; Dis - perse the gloom - y

ex - ile here Un - til the Son of God _____ ap -
give _____ the Law, In cloud, and maj - es - ty _____ and
peo - ple save, And give them vic - t'ry o'er _____ the
leads _____ on high, And close the path to mis - er -
clouds _____ of night, And death's dark shad - ows put _____ to

pear.
awe.
grave.
y.
flight.
Re - joice! Re - joice! Im - man - u -

el Shall come to thee, O Is - ra - el.

THE NATIVITY

The familiar story of the Nativity is reported only in the Gospel of Luke. None of the Apostles were present at Jesus' birth, but Luke was a physician and it has been theorized that as a physician he may have had more opportunity to minister to Jesus' mother Mary, the only person who could have known the story.

Luke adds credence to this interpretation when he prefaces his account by stating that he has set down that which was delivered to him by "eyewitnesses and ministers of the word."

And it came to pass in those days, that there went out a decree from Caesar Augustus, that all the world should be taxed . . .

And all went to be taxed, every one into his own city.

And Joseph also went up out of Galilee, out of the city of Nazareth, into Judea, unto the city of David, which is called Bethlehem (because he was of the house and lineage of David:)

To be taxed with Mary his espoused wife, being great with child.

And so it was, that, while they were there, the days were accomplished that she should be delivered.

And she brought forth her firstborn son, and wrapped him in swaddling clothes, and laid him in a manger; because there was no room for them in the inn . . .

And there were in the same country shepherds abiding in the field, keeping watch over their flock by night.

And, lo, the angel of the Lord came upon them, and the glory of the Lord shone round about them: and they were sore afraid.

And the angel said unto them, Fear not: for, behold, I bring you good tidings of great joy, which shall be to all people.

For unto you is born this day in the city of David a Saviour, which is Christ the Lord. And this shall be a sign unto you; Ye shall find the babe wrapped in swaddling clothes, lying in a manger.

And suddenly there was with the angel a multitude of the heavenly host praising, God and saying,

Glory to God in the highest, and on earth peace, good will toward men.

(Luke 2:1–14)

When Christians sought new converts among the Romans and Greeks, their most startling and likely most effective claim was that Jesus had risen after death. Announcing a virgin birth might have stirred some curiosity, but it had been claimed before. The claim that someone was the Son of God was also a very familiar one, especially to the Greeks, whose gods were reported to have wed many nubile mortals and left their mythology littered with offspring—the most prominent being the warrior Achilles.

Resurrection was relatively rarer. Easter, therefore, was the most important holiday during the first five hundred years of the Christian church, and the church assigned Christ's Nativity Day to December 25 only to compete with the popular Roman holy day devoted to Mithra.

The Nativity still didn't generate public interest. Its homey story, as told by Luke, lacked the majesty and awe needed to give the day importance as a meaningful religious festival, so the church simply adopted pagan rituals to try to popularize the holiday. Pagan rituals and decorations were allowed, as long as their purpose was bent to the ultimate good of honoring Jesus.

By A.D. 1000, Barbarian conquerors ruled much of Europe; though many had been converted to Christianity, older celebrations were maintained alongside new Christian holidays.

Some of the old Roman cities and a number of new ones began to come alive as commercial centers. Cities did not enforce the restrictions often found in the countryside, and what had once been religious celebrations now took on a more secular character.

Renewed trade at the end of the Dark Ages enriched both kings and merchants, and holiday celebrations became occasions to display their wealth and power. During the next three hundred years, life became easier and people focused on their own enjoyment. The somber Easter holiday provided little opportunity for revelry, but the agricultural conditions that originally endowed December with a natural opportunity for festivities were still operating.

December was after the harvest and there was more free time for celebrating. The herds had been reduced to the number that could be maintained on the food stored for the winter, and there was plenty of meat for feasting. The grain harvest had been fermenting and there was fresh brew. The darkening days were giving over to days with more hours of sunlight. Recognizing this, many kings, like Charlemagne of the Holy Roman Empire and later William the Conqueror, chose Christmas as their Coronation Day.

With increased wealth, the celebrations became more elaborate. Though the Church did not approve, the kings and the people wanted to turn Christmas into a fun time. Tournaments and jousts were arranged, and knights with entourages of heralds and pages would come, parading in their colors through the castle grounds. They were often accompanied by minstrels whose playing and singing added to the festive atmosphere. Kings often demanded gifts from their subjects, and land-owning nobles did the same from their serfs. Ancient traditions of dressing up in disguise and doing mischief were revived, and plays and performances were given. Celebration was in the air!

PROCLAMATION CAROLS

Four of the nativity carols—''O Come All Ye Faithful,'' ''Joy to the World,'' ''Hark! The Herald Angels Sing,'' and ''Angels We Have Heard on High''—proclaim the birth of Jesus. None of them contain any of the imagery that we associate with Christmas today. There are no mentions of trees, wreaths, presents, or children. These proclamation carols come to us from eighteenth-century England, where Christmas was once again acknowledged as a joyous time, and thus have the aura of celebration in their words and music. Some originated elsewhere, but the versions with which we are familiar passed through English hands before arriving on American shores.

In the seventeenth century, England was under the rule of Protestant fundamentalists who banned the celebration of Christmas. They felt that Christmas celebrations focused too much attention on saints and included loathsome pagan practices. By the eighteenth century the ban was lifted, but it would be another hundred years before Christmas would become the happy, fun-filled holiday that we know today. It took Clement Moore's "A Visit from St. Nicholas" (" 'Twas the night before Christmas, and all through the house . . .") and Charles Dickens's *A Christmas Carol*, combined with the new widespread prosperity of late nineteenth-century Victorian England, to bring about the type of Christmas celebration we know today.

CAROLS

O Come All Ye Faithful
(Adeste Fideles)

The background of this beloved carol is particularly confusing. For many years it was believed that "Adeste Fideles" had been a seventeenth-century hymn sung throughout France and Germany at the processional of the midnight mass on Christmas Eve. Originally it took its name from that occasion and was known as "The Midnight Mass." But more recent research has uncovered a labyrinth of a tale about its origins.

The Europeans on the continent may have known "Adeste Fideles" as "The Midnight Mass," but in England the hymn was scarcely known at all—even though it had been written by two Englishmen. When the hymn first appeared in England, it was thought to be of Portuguese origin, and was called "The Portuguese Hymn." Since England had rejected papal authority and broken with the Roman Catholic church, there were few places in England where Catholics could gather to celebrate their religion. One of these few was the chapel at the Portuguese embassy in London. There, for the first time, the English became aware of this lovely hymn and quite naturally assumed that it had been composed in Portugal.

In truth, it was brought back to the Portuguese embassy by English pilgrims after a visit to Douay, a Roman Catholic center for Englishmen in northern France. It was from this source that the English-speaking world also received the Douay version of the Old Testament, the version still used in English-speaking Catholic churches.

In residence at Douay was an Englishman, John Wade, working as a copyist and music teacher, who first wrote the Latin verses of "Adeste Fideles" in 1731. Whether he found the verses elsewhere and set them down in his own hand or wrote them himself is not certain, but most scholars credit him with authorship. So it was an Englishman, working in France, writing in Latin, who created one of the most beloved of all carols and passed it on to the English-speaking world through the Portuguese embassy!

Some believe that Wade wrote the tune as well. Others credit it to John Reading, the organist at England's Winchester Cathedral, and date it to 1760.

A third Englishman, Frederick Oakeley, provided the English words to three of the eight Latin verses in 1852 and turned "Adeste Fideles" into "O Come All Ye Faithful." He had originally tried to translate the hymn into English in 1841, but that version, entitled "Ye Faithful Approach Ye," failed to catch on. The words "O come," beckoning to everyone, were needed to induce English churchgoers to prick up their ears and take the hymn to their hearts. And so there is a triple English parentage for what had once been regarded as "The Portuguese Hymn."

O Come All Ye Faithful

By
JOHN FRANCIS WADE

Moderately

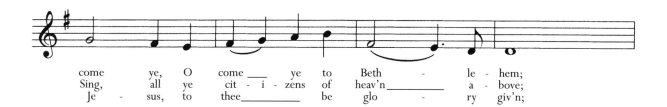

1. O come all ye faith - ful, joy -ful and tri - um - phant, O
sing, choirs of an - gels, sing with ex - ul - ta - tions.
3. Yea, Lord, we greet thee, born this hap -py morn - ing

come ye, O come ___ ye to Beth - le - hem;
Sing, all ye cit - i - zens of heav'n _____ a - bove;
Je - sus, to thee _____ be glo - ry giv'n;

Come and be - hold Him born the king of an - gels;
Glo - ry to God _____ in ___ the ___ high ___ est; } O
Word of the Fa - ther, now in flesh ap - pear - ing; }

come, let us a - dore Him, O come, let us a - dore Him, O

1.2. ———— 3.

come, let us a - dore Him: __ Christ, _____ the Lord! 2. O Lord!

Joy to the World

Here is a Nativity carol announcing that the Lord is come, but without a single reference to Christmas or any Christmas imagery. It reveals that back in 1719, when "Joy to the World" was written, people did not celebrate the way we do today,

The words to this popular carol are by Isaac Watts, the founder of English hymn writing and the author of more than six hundred hymns. Watts was the son of a deacon and when he was fifteen years old, he commented to his father about the sad state of the congregation's singing. His father challenged him to write better hymns, and Isaac's first attempts were immediate successes with his father's congregation.

He was forty-five when he published *The Psalms of David,* putting the psalms in modern English and adding Christian symbolism to the Old Testament text. This book contains a reworking of all of David's psalms as contained in the Bible. The inspiration for "Joy to the World" came from Psalm 98, which contains the phrase "Make a joyful noise unto the Lord, all the earth."

Originally Watts began the hymn with the words "Joy to the earth"—which has greater kinship with its original inspiration. Watts later changed it to more clearly refer to the whole world. It was written at a time when interest in religion had waned in England. Watts's words express his missionary zeal to convince those whose faith had lapsed that the Lord's coming meant redemption.

While the words are clearly traceable to Watts, the origin of the melody is a more complicated story. The words were published with the present tune by Lowell Mason, an American, in 1830. On the title page, Mason had printed "From George Frederick Handel." For over one hundred years, most people believed that the tune had come from the great composer, although no one thought Handel had written the music specifically for these verses.

Today there are two schools of thought: One set of musicologists feels that there isn't a single musical phrase in the entire carol that can be directly attributed to Handel's work. Another set of musicologists traces the first four notes in the key of D ("Joy to the World") to the first four notes of the *Messiah*'s chorus, "Lift Up Your Heads." They also cite the seven notes of "heaven and nature sing" as similar to the *Messiah*'s tenor solo "Comfort Ye My People."

But four notes here and seven there do not satisfy the first group of musicologists, who think either that Mason was trying to perpetrate a hoax or that he took his inspiration from Handel. Though he wrote it himself, he would not take credit for something that he genuinely felt had been inspired by the master.

The latter explanation seems more likely. The modest Mason is known to have written other music that was published anonymously, and Handel had always been his idol.

JOY TO THE WORLD

Words by ISAAC WATTS
Music by GEORGE F. HANDEL

Maestoso

1. Joy to the world! the Lord has come: Let earth re - ceive her King; Let ev - 'ry heart pre - pare Him room, And heav'n and na - ture sing, And heav'n and na - ture sing, And heav'n, and heav'n and na - ture sing.

2. Joy to the world! the Sav - ior reigns: Let men their songs em - ploy, While fields and floods, rocks, hills and plains, Re - peat the sound - ing joy, Re - peat the sound - ing joy, Re - peat, re - peat the sound - ing joy.

3. No more let sin and sor - row grow, Nor thorns in - fest the ground; He comes to make His bless - ings flow Far as the curse is found, Far as the curse is found, Far as, far as the curse is found.

4. He rules the world with truth and grace, And makes the na - tion prove The glo - ries of His right - eous - ness And won - ders of His love, And won - ders of His love, And won - ders, won - ders of His love.

Hark! The Herald Angels Sing

Although "Hark! The Herald Angels Sing" shares the celebratory mood of other proclamation carols, it was not written for Christmas. Originally it was intended as a hymn of the Incarnation, when God assumed a human nature. Religious scholars feel that this refers to the moment when Mary conceived, and not the moment of Jesus' birth. So it was intended to be sung nine months before Christmas.

Written by Charles Wesley, the founder of the Methodist church and the author of some 6,500 hymns, and inspired by the exultant pealing of the church bells on Christmas morning in 1730, the original words were:

> *Hark, how all the welkin rings,*
> *"Glory to the King of Kings,*
> *Peace on earth and mercy mild,*
> *God and sinners reconciled."*
> *Joyful all ye nations, rise,*
> *Join the triumph of the skies,*
> *Universal nature say,*
> *"Christ the Lord is born today."*

Welkin means "the vault of heaven."

His friend and co-worker in the Methodist cause, George Whitfield, changed the words to the better-known second version when he published them in 1753. For the next 120 years, the words were sung to a variety of melodies by different congregations.

The ensuing changes are subtle, but they alter the meaning of the carol. In the original version, the emphasis is on God Himself. In the version most frequently sung today, the emphasis is more clearly on the newborn holy child.

In 1840, the composer Felix Mendelssohn was asked to write a piece of music for a festival at Leipzig to celebrate the four-hundredth anniversary of Gutenberg's invention of the printing press. Mendelssohn's work was entitled *Festgesang*. It was an orchestral work with no words. The second chorus of the work, entitled "God Is Light," evoked a great deal of favorable comment. Mendelssohn agreed with many who felt that the second section was admirably suited for voice.

In 1855, John Cummings, an organist at Waltham Abbey in England, wed Wesley's words to Mendelssohn's music for the first time. He published the work the following year and bequeathed to us one of the most beloved of all Christmas carols.

HARK! THE HERALD ANGELS SING

Words by CHARLES WESLEY
Music by FELIX MENDELSSOHN

Expressively

1. Hark! the her - ald an - gels sing,___ "Glo - ry to the new - born King!
2. Christ, by high - est heav'n a - dored; __ Christ the ev - er - last - ing Lord;
3. Hail! the heav'n born Prince of Peace! __ Hail! the Son of Right - eous - ness!

Peace on earth, and mer - cy mild, __ God and sin - ners re - con - ciled."
Late in time be - hold him come,__ Off - spring of the fa - vored one.
Light and life to all he brings, _ Ris'n with heal - ing in His wings.

Joy - ful, all ye na - tions rise,___ Join the tri - umph of the skies;___
Veiled in flesh, the God - head see; ___ Hail th'in - car - nate De - i - ty ____
Mild He lays His glo - ry by, ____ Born that man no more may die: ___

With th'an - gel - ic host pro - claim, "Christ is ___ born in Beth - le - hem."
Pleased, as man with men to dwell, Je - sus, __ our Im - man - u - el!
Born to raise the sons of earth, Born to ___ give them sec - ond birth.

Hark the her - ald an - gels sing, "Glo - ry ___ to the new - born King!"
Hark the her - ald an - gels sing, "Glo - ry ___ to the new - born King!"
Hark the her - ald an - gels sing, "Glo - ry ___ to the new - born King!"

Angels We Have Heard on High

"Angels We Have Heard on High" was published as a poem in a newspaper on Christmas Eve in 1816. Though the Bible says that the angels *said* "Glory to God in the highest," an oral tradition has been passed down the centuries that the angels *sang* those words to the shepherds. Poet James Montgomery takes the side of the singing angels.

Three years after its publication in the newspaper, the carol was republished in a collection of poetry. At that time it was set to music. Some musicologists trace the music in the verse to a lighthearted French carol and the music to the "*Gloria*" chorus to a medieval Latin chorale. The blend of two such disparate types of music may be what gives this carol its unique appeal, almost as if the two different Christmas traditions—the merry and the solemn—were blended together in one.

ANGELS WE HAVE HEARD ON HIGH

Joyously

Traditional French-English

1. An - gels we have heard on high, Sweet - ly sing - ing o'er the plains;
2. Shep - herds, why this ju - bi - lee? Why your joy - ous songs pro - long?
3. Come to Beth - le - hem and see Him whose birth the an - gels sing;

And the moun - tains in re - ply Ech - o - ing their joy - ous strains.
What the glad - some ti - dings be Which in - spire your heav'n - ly song?
Come a - dore on bend - ed knee Christ, the Lord, our new - born King.

Glo - ri - a

in ex - cel - sis De - o, Glo -

ri - a in ex - cel - sis De - o!

The First Noel

The word *Noel* came into the English language from the French. In French it is used to refer both to Christmas itself and to replace the word *carol*. Originally, it may have been the Latin word *natalis*, which means "birthday."

When the word entered into English usage, it was written *Nowell*. The English supposed it was a contraction of the phrase that the angels spoke when they wanted to calm the shepherds: "now all is well."

The words, which probably date from the seventeenth century, were published ten years before the music in a collection of carols from 1823.

Clearly they were not written by a poet. They are awkwardly phrased ("This child truly there born he was") and border on being repetitious ("And there it did both stop and stay"). It is unlikely that the words were written by the clergy. The Bible never mentions that shepherds actually saw the star, as is claimed in the second verse. All of this suggests that the words may have accrued through usage as common folk sang them year after year, without anyone writing them down until long after they were well known and more difficult to correct.

The melody was first reported in Sandys's book of carols in 1833, but is likely a folk tune from the thirteenth or fourteenth century. Thus, this may be the most ancient of all the carols in this book.

THE FIRST NOEL

Moderately

Traditional

O Little Town of Bethlehem

In 1865, Phillip Brooks, the rector of the Episcopalian Church of the Holy Trinity in Philadelphia, was visiting the Holy Land. In his diary he wrote:

Before dark we rode out of town to the field where they say the shepherds saw the star. It is a fenced piece of ground with a cave in it, in which, strangely enough, they put the shepherds . . . somewhere in those fields we rode through, the shepherds must have been. As we passed, the shepherds were still "keeping watch over their flocks," or leading them home to fold.

That night Brooks, a very devout man, attended services in the Church of the Nativity from ten at night until three in the morning.

I remember especially on Christmas Eve when I was standing in the old church in Bethlehem, close to the spot where Jesus was born, when the whole church was ringing hour after hour with the splendid hymns of praise to God, how again and again it seemed as if I could hear voices I know well, telling each other of the "Wonderful Night" of the Saviour's birth, as I heard them a year before.

The experience of that journey stayed with him and, three years later, when his Sunday school class asked him for a Christmas song, he brought his memories of the stillness of that night to a poem.

In the words that would become "O Little Town of Bethlehem," one can discern a theme not apparent in earlier carols. By 1868, the Christmas revival was in full swing and our writer is more concerned that the *spirit* of Christmas should enter into everyone's heart than he is with praising God or describing the manger scene.

Brooks finished the verses about one week before Christmas. He asked Lewis H. Redner, the church organist, for a tune. Redner was a local businessman who was particularly busy at Christmas. Although he devoted what time he could, he was unable to devise a suitable melody. But he claimed that as he slept on Christmas Eve, he heard "an angel strain" in his dream. He awoke to write it down and arrange it in time for the Christmas service. For the rest of his life, Redner would describe the melody as "a gift from heaven."

O Little Town of Bethlehem

Words by PHILIPS BROOKS
Music by LEWIS H. REDNER

Slowly

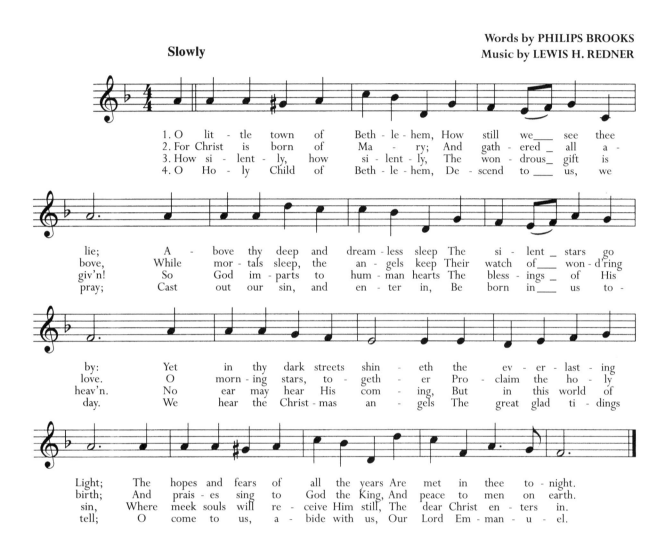

1. O lit-tle town of Beth-le-hem, How still we____ see thee lie;
2. For Christ is born of Ma - ry; And gath-ered_ all a-bove,
3. How si - lent - ly, how si - lent - ly, The won - drous_ gift is giv'n!
4. O Ho - ly Child of Beth - le - hem, De - scend to ___ us, we pray;

Yet in thy dark streets shin - eth the ev - er - last - ing
A - bove thy deep and dream-less sleep The si - lent_ stars go by:
While mor - tals sleep, the an - gels keep Their watch of___ won - d'ring love.
So God im - parts to hum - an hearts The bless - ings_ of His heav'n.
Cast out our sin, and en - ter in, Be born in___ us to-

Light; The hopes and fears of all the years Are met in thee to - night.
birth; And prais - es sing to God the King, And peace to men on earth.
sin, Where meek souls will re - ceive Him still, The dear Christ en - ters in.
tell; O come to us, a - bide with us, Our Lord Em - man - u - el.

Silent Night

"Silent Night," perhaps the most beloved of all carols, was written by an alcoholic priest and organist who was supposed to be at a different church in another town. In fact, the song was hurriedly written on December 23, with no help from a broken organ. The Lord works in mysterious ways.

The writer of the words, Joseph Mohr, was raised by priests who, recognizing his fine tenor voice, trained him for the priesthood. In 1818, Mohr was twenty-six years old and working as a priest at the Church of St. Nikola in Obendorf, Austria. The church organ's bellows had rusted and the organ could not be played. Mohr was upset that there might be no music for the Christmas Eve service. He discussed it with the man who usually played the organ at St. Nikola, Franz Gruber.

Gruber had inherited his jobs as schoolteacher, sexton, and organist in the town of Arnsdorf by marrying the widow of the man who formerly held those positions. On this day he was supposed to be tending to his Arnsdorf duties some miles away, but hoping to collect two fees, he assigned those chores to his stepson and went to St. Nikola.

Knowing the organ was in need of repair, Gruber had brought his guitar. He set Mohr's verses for guitar, tenor, baritone, and children's chorus. It was performed for the first time on that Christmas Eve.

When Karl Mauracher, the repairman, came to fix the organ, Gruber played "Silent Night" for him. Through his contacts, the carol was performed by various family singing groups touring Austria. A publisher in Dresden heard it, wrote it down from memory, and published it, "author unknown." Its fame grew, but no one stepped forward to claim authorship.

King Friedrich Wilhelm IV of Prussia requested that his *Kappelmeister* (choirmaster) perform it. The *Kappelmeister*, believing that the author was Franz Joseph Haydn's younger brother Michael, sent to Michael's old school in Salzburg for a copy. In one of those wondrous coincidences or divine interventions, the task of going through Michael Haydn's papers was given to none other than Franz Gruber's son, a student at the school. The son informed the choirmaster of the true authorship, and his father wrote out a new arrangement for a small orchestra to be played for the king. At Friedrich Wilhelm IV's request, it was performed for him every Christmas thereafter.

But not everyone was willing to acknowledge Gruber's claim. Mohr, who moved from one parish to another, due to his alcoholism, could not be located for corroboration. Mohr died in 1848 and was not available when the government sponsored an investigation to determine the true authorship of what had become a famous carol.

Gruber died in 1863. It was not until 1867, in a handbook about the Pongau district in which Obendorf is located, that there was official acknowledgment of the authorship by Mohr and Gruber.

Silent Night

Words by JOSEPH MOHR
Music by FRANZ GRUBER

Calmly, with reverence

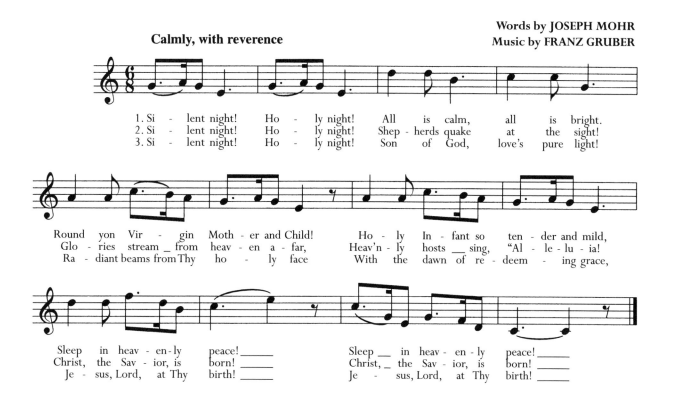

1. Si - lent night! Ho - ly night! All is calm, all is bright.
2. Si - lent night! Ho - ly night! Shep - herds quake at the sight!
3. Si - lent night! Ho - ly night! Son of God, love's pure light!

Round yon Vir - gin Moth - er and Child! Ho - ly In - fant so ten - der and mild,
Glo - ries stream _ from heav - en a - far, Heav'n - ly hosts _ sing, "Al - le - lu - ia!
Ra - diant beams from Thy ho - ly face With the dawn of re - deem - ing grace,

Sleep in heav - en - ly peace! _____ Sleep _ in heav - en - ly peace! _____
Christ, the Sav - ior, is born! _____ Christ, _ the Sav - ior, is born! _____
Je - sus, Lord, at Thy birth! _____ Je - sus, Lord, at Thy birth! _____

O Holy Night

Almost all of our favorite Christmas carols were written for chorus and are usually sung by groups. But one, "O Holy Night," was written as a solo; today it has become the most popular of all Christmas solo music.

Though immensely popular for the previous seventy-five years, in the 1930s this deeply moving carol was assailed by the clergy in France (where it was written) as having a "total absence of the spirit of religion."

The original French words were written by Placide Cappeau, a wine merchant near Avignon in the Rhône valley. On December 3, 1847, Cappeau was on a train bound for Paris. He had been asked by the local parish priest to write a Christmas poem and take it to the friend of another townsman—Adolphe Adam, a composer of ballets (*Giselle*) and operas. During the train ride, inspiration struck Cappeau and he wrote the poem he entitled *"Cantique de Noel."*

As requested, he took the poem to Adam, who set it to music over the next few days. Cappeau returned with the requested carol and it was first presented at the local midnight mass on Christmas Eve in 1847. Its fame spread quickly and an English translation followed a few years later.

The French clergy did not object to the carol as much as to the carol's authors. Adam was regarded as a composer of secular theater music and, as such, unsuitable to be the composer of a religious work. In addition, neither Adam nor Cappeau was a practicing Christian. Cappeau was a radical freethinker who repudiated his *"Cantique de Noel"* in 1876.

But if one knows nothing about its authorship, the soaring melody and words of rejoicing of "O Holy Night" surely seem to have been touched by grace. The spirit of the nativity infuses its verses—"O holy night," "O night divine,"—and the message of peace and redemption is spelled out for all to hear.

Of course, we appreciate it in its English translation by John Dwight, a co-founder of the Harvard Musical Association. Dwight appears to have caught the spirit of Adam's and Cappeau's inspiration. But a frequently cited tale about the carol causes one to wonder whether the inspiration and the feeling in the music aren't sufficient by themselves. On Christmas Eve in 1870, during the Franco-Prussian War, French and German soldiers were entrenched outside Paris. Despite the day's vicious fighting, a French soldier left his trench during a lull and sang Adam's "Cantique de Noel." The German soldiers were so moved that they did not attack, and in fact, a German responded with a Lutheran hymn.

The Franco-Prussian incident is fervent testimony to Cappeau's words:

Truly He taught us to love one another;
His law is love and His gospel is peace.

O Holy Night

Words and Music by
ADOLPHE ADAM

Slowly and majestically

1. O ho - ly night___ the stars are bright - ly shin - ing, It is the
2. Led by the light___ of faith se - rene - ly beam - ing, With glow - ing
3. Tru - ly He taught us to love one an - oth - er - er, His law is

night of the dear Sav - ior's birth; Long lay the world___ in sin and er - ror
hearts by His cra - dle we stand; So led by light of a star sweet - ly
love, and His gos - pel is peace; Chains shall He break for the slave is our

pin - ing, Till He ap - peared and the soul felt its worth. A
gleam - ing, Here came the wise men from O - ri - ent land. The
broth - er, And in His name all op - pres - sion shall cease. Sweet

thrill of hope the wea - ry soul re - joic - es, For yon - der breaks a
King of Kings lay thus in low - ly man - ger, In all our tri - als
hymns of joy in grate - ful cho - rus raise we, Let all with - in us

new and glo - rious morn; ___ Fall on your knees, Oh, hear____ the an - gel
born to be our friend; ___ He knows our need, Our weak - ness is no
praise His ho - ly name;___ Christ is the Lord, Oh, praise___ His name for -

voic - es! O night_____ di - vine,_____ O night_____ when Christ was
stran - ger Be - hold_____ your King, _____ be - fore _____ Him low - ly
ev - er! His pow'r ____ and glo - ry ev - er - more pro -

1.2.

born! O night, O ho - ly night O night di - vine!
bend! Be - hold your King be - fore Him low - ly bend!
claim! His

3.

pow'r and glo - ry___ ev - er - more pro - claim!

ST. FRANCIS AND THE FAMILY CHRISTMAS

In the Middle Ages, Christmas was celebrated with pageants in town centers and royally sponsored plays, tournaments, jousts, masques, and dances. Taking note of this trend toward secularizing the holiday, the church drew back and tried to refocus parishioners on a more solemn religious interpretation of Christmas. They restricted Christmas church music to ancient hymns and forbade the use of gestures and costumes—all too reminiscent of the Christmastime celebrations going on in the towns and royal courts.

For St. Francis, the ''little child'' was the essence of the spiritual message he wished to preach. About two weeks before Christmas 1223, he asked a friend to prepare a living crèche at Greccio in the Umbrian hill country of Italy. He hoped to inspire others to think about the infant Jesus as central to the message of the church. He specifically requested that the infant be shown in the manger, with Mary and Joseph watching over him. Though Luke's Gospel does not mention any animals at the Nativity crèche, St. Francis loved animals too much to exclude them, he specified an ox and an ass. The presence of an ox and an ass had existed in popular folklore, probably based on another portion of Isaiah (1:3):

The ox knoweth his owner, and the ass his master's crib: but Israel doth not know, my people doth not consider.

At a time when the church had forbidden masques and plays, the Nativity scene was quite a break with church doctrine. The human figures were merely models, though the animals were alive.

The living Nativity scene was prepared so that St. Francis might say a mass on Christmas Eve. The people gathered and, as St. Bonaventure reported:

Greccio was transformed almost into a second Bethlehem and that wonderful night seemed like the fullest day to both man and beast for the joy they felt at the renewing of the mystery.

St. Francis's biographer, Thomas of Celano, writes:

The men and women of the neighborhood, as best they could, prepared candles and torches to brighten the night. . . . The crib was made ready, hay was brought, the ox and ass were led to the spot. . . . The crowds drew near and rejoiced in the novelty of the celebration. Their voices resounded . . . and the rocky cliff echoed the jubilant outburst. And they sang in praise of God and the whole night rang with exultation.

Live reproductions of the Nativity story had been performed in churches in England and in Germany before. In various parts of Europe, productions featuring scenes from the Nativity tale had been mounted on wagons and pulled through the town—a tableau of the entire story. But something of St. Francis's simple passion was now a part of it, and his vision was infectious. He created what would become a tradition. Not only did it give rise to other towns presenting living Nativity scenes, but it also led to the carved miniature manger scenes.

Simple wooden cribs adorned farmhouses while the nobles, who had taken Christmas celebrating to excesses in the past, were bound to take the Nativity scene along the same opulent pathways. Artists were commissioned to make elaborate cribs of gold, studded with precious jewels. Figures of the wise men and then shepherds were added. Angels were added. Costumes were fashioned from imported satins and silks.

Somehow St. Francis's message got through, as well. Franciscan friars carried the word into northern lands. Among German tribes, whose culture was more family oriented, the idea of a celebration centered on the Holy Family planted its firmest roots.

The family Christmas, one in which a child played a major part, became central to the Christmas tradition, and remains so today.

CRADLE-ROCKING CAROLS

While some celebrants may have emphasized the majesty and power of Christ's appearance on earth, the Germans emphasized the fact that He arrived as a baby and as part of a family. This led to a German tradition of carving wooden toys for Christmas gifts. The American emphasis on Christmas as a holiday that focuses on children and family can be traced to eighteenth-century German immigrants to America as well as indirectly through England, after German-born Prince Albert's marriage to Queen Victoria.

Another German Christmas custom, although it did not survive the centuries, did bequeath us a legacy of gentle Christmas carols. In fourteenth-century Germany and Austria, there arose a custom called *Kindelwiegen*. During the Christmas season, religious plays were enacted in which one priest took the part of Joseph and, while the choir sang, another impersonated the Virgin Mary rocking the cradle in which the infant Jesus lay. The choir sang in rhythms harmonious with the rocking of the cradle. Influenced by Franciscan missionaries, Germans thought of Jesus as a universal child or little brother figure. This did not sit well with official doctrine about Jesus and, in the sixteenth century, met with church opposition. As a result the plays and the practice of *Kindelwiegen* disappeared from public festivals. But the "Christmas cradle songs" or "lullaby carols" planted deep cultural roots and are reflected in two of our most beloved carols, "Away in a Manger" and "What Child Is This?"

THE MYSTERY PLAYS

St. Francis had provided the church with a counterweight attraction to the tournaments and spectacles of the manor. The Nativity pageants often involved a series of scenes: the Annunciation followed by the refusal at the inn, the birth in the stable, the angels revealing the birth to the shepherds, the arrival of the Magi, and so on. Each scene might be mounted on a horsecart and paraded through the town. These scenes retold the old familiar story in ways that made their meaning more vivid.

In medieval times such plays were used to dramatize a great many Bible stories. The usual practice was to assign one scene to each guild—and a particular guild would usually be assigned a scene related to its craft. The shipwrights might be asked to show the scene of Noah and the construction of the ark, while the goldsmiths might be asked to create the scene of the Magi who brought gold to the infant Jesus. Only the Nativity pageants were called "Mystery Plays"—because they were the only plays to depict the Holy Mystery of Jesus' birth.

As the guilds became more involved with the plays, the plays became more secularized. The earliest plays, often performed inside the churches, were accompanied with liturgical music. But as the plays moved into the town squares, the language moved toward the vernacular and the music was more likely to be borrowed from traditional folk songs set with new lyrics.

The plays created striking pictures of biblical stories. And now, accompanied with carols—songs in the vernacular of the everyday people, songs usually filled with joy—the plays, though biblical in subject matter, became less solemn and less didactic. This in turn led to the carols being composed to describe the scene as it was staged, rather than the original Gospel story. It is from this tradition that we get the "Coventry Carol."

CAROLS

Away in a Manger

"Away in a Manger" was written by an unknown Pennsylvanian in 1885. In 1887, James Ramsay Murray, a music editor with a company in Cincinnati, republished it in a book titled *Dainty Songs for Little Lads and Lasses for Use in Kindergarten, School and Home*; he called it "Luther's Cradle Hymn" and beneath the title it read, "Composed by Martin Luther for his children and still sung by German mothers to their little ones."

Murray may have been trying to hype sales, or it might have been an honest mistake. Previously, the words had been published in two separate books about Luther. In one book—T. B. Stoke's *Luther at Home*, published in 1872—the text reads, "Luther's carol for Christmas, written for his own child, Hans, is still sung."

Luther did write words for many carols, one of which has the opening line, "Away there in the manger a little Infant lies," but the remainder of the verses are not the same as the more familiar carol we know and love.

Whoever wrote the words, the context of the second verse may seem confused. Just who is in the cradle? It is supposed to be Lord Jesus. But who is in the sky? If Jesus is *in* the cradle, why ask him to stay *by* the cradle? It is likely that the second verse reflects a modern mother rocking her baby to sleep. She relates the story of the Nativity to her infant and then asks Jesus to watch over her child. A third verse was added some years after the first two were published and is almost certainly not by the same author.

Soon after the words were first published, they were set to a hymn—"St. Kilda" by J. E. Clark. In the century since the poem was first published, it has been set to forty-one different melodies. The version we sing today is the one published as "Luther's Cradle Hymn" by Murray. Most scholars think it may have originally been a German folk song.

AWAY IN A MANGER

Tenderly

by MARTIN LUTHER

1. A - way in a man - ger, No crib for a bed, The
2. The cat - tle are low - ing, The poor Ba - by wakes, But
3. Be near me, Lord Je - sus, I ask Thee to stay, Close

lit - tle Lord Je - sus Laid down His sweet head; The
lit - tle Lord Je - sus No cry - ing He makes; I
by me for - ev - er, And love me, I pray; Bless

stars in the sky _____ Looked down where He lay, The
love Thee, Lord Je - sus Look down from the sky, And
all the dear chil - dren In Thy ten - der care, And

lit - tle Lord Je - sus A - sleep on the hay.
stay by my cra - dle, Till morn - ing is nigh.
take us to heav - en, To live with Thee there.

What Child Is This?

The lyrics to the other favorite cradle carol, "What Child Is This?," were written during the reign of Queen Victoria by an English hymnist, William Chatterton Dix, who earned his living as an insurance company executive.

Written in the latter half of the nineteenth century, this carol begins to reflect some of what we think of as traditional Christmas imagery: the kings, the shepherds, and even the ox and ass. In the Bible, no ox, ass, or shepherds are included in the description of what happened in the stable. This reflects the emerging influence of the kind of homey Christmas envisioned by St. Francis, and the roots of our more modern, secular, family Christmas celebrations, as distinct from austere religious church rites.

Dix set his words to a very old tune, "Greensleeves," which is rumored to have been written by Henry VIII. The first registration of the music is in 1580 by Richard Jones, and it had the love lyrics known to every folk song devotee:

> *Alas, my love, you do me wrong*
>
> *To cast me off discourteously,*
>
> *For I have loved you so long,*
>
> *Delighting in your company*
>
> *Greensleeves was all my joy,*
>
> *And Greensleeves was my delight,*
>
> *Greensleeves was my heart of gold,*
>
> *And who but my Lady Greensleeves?*

The tune for "Greensleeves" may have come from an even older traditional folk song. By 1580, the tune was already so popular that it is mentioned in two of Shakespeare's plays. Over the years it has been used repeatedly, at least once as a drinking song and another time as a prisoner's lament. Today the music is occasionally heard as a folk song, but almost universally heard at Christmastime, with Dix's words, rocking the infant Jesus to sleep.

WHAT CHILD IS THIS?

Moderately   Traditional

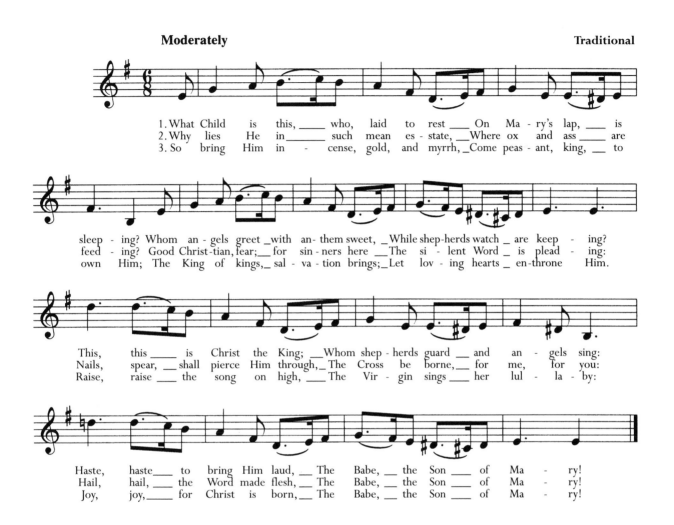

1. What Child is this, ____ who, laid to rest ____ On Ma - ry's lap, ____ is
2. Why lies He in_____ such mean es - state, __Where ox and ass ____ are
3. So bring Him in - cense, gold, and myrrh, __Come peas - ant, king, __ to

sleep - ing? Whom an - gels greet _with an - them sweet, _While shep-herds watch _ are keep - ing?
feed - ing? Good Christ-tian, fear; __ for sin - ners here __The si - lent Word _ is plead - ing:
own Him; The King of kings,_ sal - va - tion brings;_Let lov - ing hearts _ en-throne Him.

This, this ____ is Christ the King; __Whom shep-herds guard __ and an - gels sing:
Nails, spear, __ shall pierce Him through,_The Cross be borne, __ for me, for you:
Raise, raise ____ the song on high, ____The Vir - gin sings ____ her lul - la - by:

Haste, haste____ to bring Him laud, __ The Babe, __ the Son ____ of Ma - ry!
Hail, hail, ____ the Word made flesh, __ The Babe, __ the Son ____ of Ma - ry!
Joy, joy,____ for Christ is born,__ The Babe, __ the Son ____ of Ma - ry!

Coventry Carol

One of the few Mystery Play carols to survive is the "Coventry Carol," although it is also classified as a lullaby carol, a close relative of cradle-rocking carols. It is from the Pageant of the Shearmen and Tailors, written in the fifteenth century, which describes Herod's slaughter of the Innocents and is sung by the women of Bethlehem just before the soldiers arrive. The earliest known version is dated 1591, but it is assumed that it dates back another hundred years at least. This original version differs only slightly from the modern version.

THE COVENTRY CAROL

Tenderly
English, 16th Century

1. Lul - lay, thou lit - tle ti - ny child
2. O sis - ters too, how may we do,

by by, lul - ly lul - lay. _____ Lul -
for to pre - serve this day. _____ This

lay, thou lit - tle ti - ny child.
poor young - ling for whom we sing.

By by, lul - ly, lul - lay. _____
By by, lul - ly, lul - lay. _____

3. Herod the king,
   In his raging,
   Charged he hath this day.
   His men of might,
   In his own sight,
   All young children to slay.

4. That woe is me,
   Poor child for thee!
   And ever morn and day,
   For thy parting
   Neither say nor sing
   By by, lully lullay!

THE VISIT
OF THE MAGI

Matthew (2:1–12) tells us of the visit of the Magi. His Gospel was apparently addressed to the Jews in an effort to convince them that Jesus was the Messiah for whom they had waited for so long.

Matthew's inclusion of the story of the Magi had two apparent purposes. First, it lent credence to his claim that Jesus was the Messiah. After all, if the Magi came all the way from the East—guided by a divine star—then who are you to doubt Jesus' divinity? Second, it also represented the ascendancy of the spiritual and religious over the temporal everyday sources of power and prestige.

> Now when Jesus was born in Bethlehem of Judea in the days of Herod the king, behold, there came wise men from the east to Jerusalem,
> Saying, Where is he that is born King of the Jews? for we have seen his star in the east, and are come to worship him.

> . . . Then Herod, when he had privily called the wise men, enquired of them diligently what time the star appeared.

And he sent them to Bethlehem, and said, Go and search diligently for the young child; and when ye have found him, bring me word again, that I may come and worship him also.

When they had heard the king, they departed; and, lo, the star, which they saw in the east, went before them, till it came and stood over where the young child was.

When they saw the star, they rejoiced with exceeding great joy.

And when they were come into the house, they saw the young child with Mary his mother, and fell down, and worshipped him: and when they had opened their treasures, they presented unto him gifts; gold, and frankincense, and myrrh.

And being warned of God in a dream that they should not return to Herod, they departed into their own country another way.

To the early church, January 6, traditionally the day of Jesus' baptism by John the Baptist, was in fact the "true" birthday of Jesus—the day he was born into the church. Many in the Eastern Orthodox church continue to celebrate January 6 as the date of Jesus' birth. In addition, it was traditionally the day of Jesus' first miracle, turning water into wine. Needing a holiday to compete with the pagan river god ceremonies of the Egyptians and Greeks, the church emphasized Jesus' associations with water on January 6, and the holiday became known as his birthday—at least in the Eastern Orthodox church.

Two hundred years later, when the cult of Mithra had been proclaimed the official religion of Rome, and Mithra's day was being celebrated on December 25, the Western church needed a holiday to counter this new threat. The Magi had come from the East—the home of Mithra—and if they accepted Jesus' divinity, then that was an important proof that Jesus was the more important deity. Thus, in the West, the visit of the Magi became more important than Jesus' baptism as a way of countering the influence of Mithraism. Once the meaning of Twelfth Night was fixed on the Magi, Jesus' birthday could be assigned to a different date. The Feast of the Epiphany, celebrating the visit of the Magi, became the official January 6 holiday.

The Magi brought the original Christmas gifts: gold, frankincense, and myrrh. To many, that was the sign that January 6 was the day to give presents. To this day in Spain and Mexico and in some Eastern churches, the Feast of the Epiphany is the day when gifts are exchanged.

THE EPIPHANY CAROLS

One of the all-time favorite carols, "I Saw Three Ships," is so old that it may date from a time when the Epiphany was still celebrated as the more important holiday. Over the years, that feast day and the legends surrounding Twelfth Night have inspired many carols, two of which—"I Saw Three Ships" and "We Three Kings"—remain favorites to this day.

In the Bible, the number of wise men is not specified. What is specified is the number and types of gifts that they brought—three: gold, frankincense, and myrrh. Because of the gifts, it became common to think of just three wise men.

Over the years, what the Bible called *magi,* originally a term applied to Persian astrologers, came to refer to any wise men. In time, they were referred to as kings— dramatizing that even royalty acknowledged the Son of God as their Lord.

The Feast of the Epiphany, or Twelfth Night, was once widely celebrated with the merriest of revels, bringing the holiday season to an end. In modern times it has fallen victim to industrialization, which could not tolerate two whole weeks of partying.

CAROLS

Good King Wenceslas

This carol was written for St. Stephen's Day, which falls on December 26 and celebrates the first Christian martyr. St. Stephen's Day was the first in a series of holidays leading up to the Epiphany. The song celebrates a man who, like St. Stephen, did much charitable work among the poor. It recounts a medieval legend that has no direct relationship to Christmas, and Christmas is never mentioned in the words.

Even stranger, the verses were written about a real person, but someone who was neither a king nor named Wenceslas. The man was the Duke of Bohemia, and in Bohemian the name would be translated as Vaclav. The duke was a zealous Christian, eager to convert others to his faith—by force if necessary. But he was apparently also a charitable man, whose good works were as legendary as his zealousness. He was murdered in 929 by his brother Boleslav in a palace intrigue.

The song tells a mystical legend that had been popular for hundreds of years before it was set to music. Wenceslas goes among the poor to do charitable deeds, followed by his page bearing the goods Wenceslas intends to distribute. The December weather begins to chill the page. Wenceslas suggests that the page walk in his footsteps. The page does so and is magically kept warm.

The words were written by the Reverend John Mason Neale, the warden of Sackville College in Sussex, England, in 1853. It was a time in which carol singing was undergoing a revival. The music for a collection of old carols had been republished, and Neale chose one, "*Tempus Adest Floridum,*" and set the table to it.

The carol he chose originated in the thirteenth century and freely translated means "Spring Has Now Unwrapped the Flowers." It was a carol to the springtime:

Spring has now unwrapped the flowers,

Day is fast reviving,

Life in all her growing powers,

Towards the light is striving;

Gone the iron tough of cold,

Winter time and frost time,

Seedlings working through the mold,

Now make up for lost time.

GOOD KING WENCESLAS

Words by JOHN NEALE
Music Traditional

Moderately

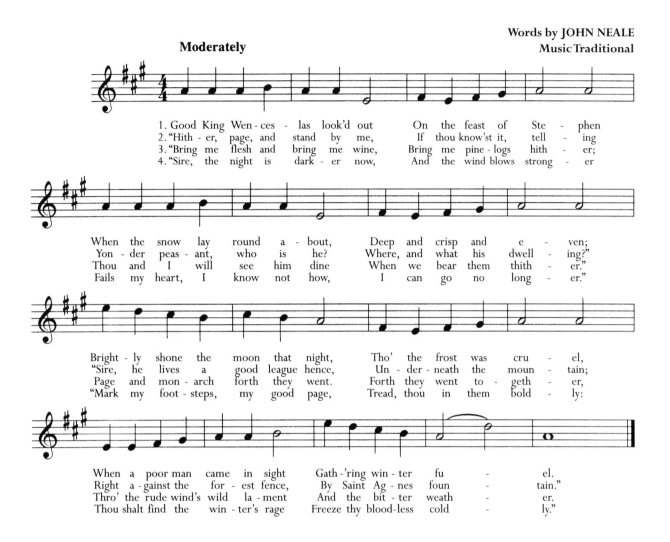

1. Good King Wen - ces - las look'd out On the feast of Ste - phen
2. "Hith - er, page, and stand by me, If thou know'st it, tell - ing
3. "Bring me flesh and bring me wine, Bring me pine - logs hith - er;
4. "Sire, the night is dark - er now, And the wind blows strong - er

When the snow lay round a - bout, Deep and crisp and e - ven;
Yon - der peas - ant, who is he? Where, and what his dwell - ing?"
Thou and I will see him dine When we bear them thith - er."
Fails my heart, I know not how, I can go no long - er."

Bright - ly shone the moon that night, Tho' the frost was cru - el,
"Sire, he lives a good league hence, Un - der - neath the moun - tain;
Page and mon - arch forth they went. Forth they went to - geth - er,
"Mark my foot - steps, my good page, Tread, thou in them bold - ly:

When a poor man came in sight Gath -'ring win - ter fu - el.
Right a - gainst the for - est fence, By Saint Ag - nes foun - tain."
Thro' the rude wind's wild la - ment And the bit - ter weath - er.
Thou shalt find the win - ter's rage Freeze thy blood-less cold - ly."

I Saw Three Ships

Well over five hundred years old, the origins of this carol have been lost. But its question-response format suggests that it had been used as a teaching device.

If you have wondered why there were three ships to bring two people to Bethlehem, it is because the carol wasn't originally written about the Virgin Mary and Jesus. The traditional story about the ships is that they were sent by the Empress Helena, mother of the Emperor Constantine, to bring the remains of the three Magi back to Constantinople. Later their remains were brought to Milan and finally, in 1162, were taken to Cologne under the orders of the Emperor Frederick Barbarossa. The song is thought to refer to the trip to Cologne; there are three ships because the original words referred to the three Magi, one aboard each ship.

The question-and-answer format of the carol and the repetitive structure may frequently be found in folk songs from medieval times. That is why scholars claim that ''I Saw Three Ships'' may be the oldest extant carol to have originated in English. It was found in Sandys's collection of carols published in 1833.

The words suggest that the carol arose among ordinary people and not from the clergy, because no ships could ever have sailed into landlocked Bethlehem! It is assumed that most clergy would have known this and that lay folk might not. Thus, both the music and the words suggest an origin among ordinary people, a merry song sung on a merry occasion.

I Saw Three Ships

Spirited

English

I saw three ships come sail - ling in, On Christ - mas Day, on Christ - mas Day; I
what was in those ships all three, On Christ - mas Day, on Christ - mas Day; And

saw three ships come sail - ling in, On Christ - mas Day in the morn - ing. And
what was in those ships all three, On Christ - mas Day in the morn - ing. The

Vir - gin Mar - y and Christ were there, On Christ - mas Day, on Christ - mas Day; The

Vir - gin Mar - y and Christ were there, On Christ - mas Day in the morn - ing.

We Three Kings

This favorite carol was written in 1857 by John Henry Hopkins, Jr., the rector of Christ Church in Williamsport, Pennsylvania. Some say it was written for a Christmas pageant to be given at the General Theological Seminary in New York City, where Hopkins was an instructor of music.

In another version of how it came to be written, Hopkins was supposed to be on his regular holiday visit with his father, an Episcopal bishop in Burlington, Vermont, when he wrote this carol for his visiting nieces and nephews.

The words are not based on any biblical text, as the Bible does not specify how many wise men visited the manger, nor does it call them kings, nor does it give them names. One would imagine that if this had been written for a pageant to be presented to scholars at a seminary, it would stay closer to biblical sources.

The description of the three kings and their names comes to us from the Venerable Bede. In 735 St. Bede retold the legend and gave the three their names and descriptions.

He described Melchior as a white-bearded old man. Melchior brought gold, the gift of royalty, to signify Jesus' kingly position on earth. Gaspar, a young man of "ruddy hue," brought frankincense, an aromatic tree bark, whose fragrance was intended to waft skyward to heaven, a sign of Jesus' unity with God. It has been suggested that the frankincense had a more practical use, to make sweet the awful smells of the manger. Balthazar is described as black complexioned, with a heavy black beard. He brought myrrh, which prefigured the death of the Son of Man. Myrrh is an unguent, used in those days to prepare bodies for burial.

Hopkins wrote many hymns and carols. In 1860 he published a collection of his work, *Carols, Hymns and Songs,* in which "We Three Kings" appeared in print for the first time. Little else that Hopkins wrote is regularly performed. Of all his work, only this one carol, which has remained a favorite for over a century, would be familiar to modern ears.

We Three Kings of Orient Are

Andante

1. *Tutti:* We three Kings of O - ri - ent are; bear - ing
2. *Melchior:* Born a king on Beth - le - hem's plain. Gold I
3. *Casper:* Frank - in - cense to of - fer have I; in - cense
4. *Balthazar:* Myrrh is mine, it's bit - ter per - fume, breathes a
5. *Tutti:* Glo - rious now be - hold Him a - rise, King and

gifts we tra - verse a - far. Field and foun - tain,
bring we to crown Him a - gain. King for - ev - er,
owns a De - i - ty high. Pray'r and prais - ing,
life of gath - er - ing gloom. Sor - rowing, sigh - ing,
God and Sac - ri - fice, Al - le - lu - ia.

moor and moun - tain fol - low - ing yon - der star.
ccas - ing nev - er. O - ver all to reign.
all men rais - ing, wor - ship Him God most high.
bleed - ing, dy - ing, seal'd in the stone - cold tomb.
Al - le - lu - ia. Earth __ to heav'n re - plies.

O _____

star of won - der, star of night, star with roy - al

beau - ty bright. West - ward lead - ing, still pro -

1.-4.   **5.**

ceed - ing guide us to the per - fect light. light.

THE MESSAGE OF CHRISTMAS

The favorite carols discussed up to this point either announce Jesus' Coming, proclaim His birth, describe the Nativity scene, or refer to the Epiphany. Only one of those carols, "Hark! The Herald Angels Sing," comes close to what we in the twenty-first century think of as the essential message of Christmas:

> And suddenly there was with the angel a multitude of the heavenly host
> praising God, and saying,
> Glory to God in the highest, and on earth peace, good will toward men.
>
> (Luke 2: 13–14)

In "Hark! The Herald Angels Sing," this message is more mellifluously rendered as "Peace on earth and mercy mild."

There have been many attempts to render this message in song. But only two examples claim our attention among the most popular carols: "God Rest Ye Merry Gentlemen," one of the oldest carols, and "It Came upon the Midnight Clear," a carol written relatively recently, in 1849.

CAROLS

God Rest Ye
Merry Gentlemen

Who were the "Merry Gentlemen"?

There weren't any. It is simply a case of a wandering comma. Originally, the words were "God rest ye merry, gentlemen." For the word *rest*, substitute the word *keep* to understand the original meaning of the song—"may God keep you merry." But the music has no pause or rest after the note on which we sing "merry." To those without a text in hand, the meaning may have been unclear. Over the years, some printers omitted the comma or moved it to appear after the word *ye*, causing some confusion.

No one knows the exact origin of this carol, but most scholars think it dates from the seventeenth century. Copies of it have been found set to a variety of different melodies, but the one that is commonly sung today is probably the oldest and most popular. It is an odd melody for a Christmas carol, because it is set in a minor key. Minor keys are most frequently associated with the blues and other jazzy music. But the song is so boisterous and jolly that it overwhelms the listener with a sense of merriment. The merriment is so pervasive that it may be easy to overlook the fact that the words are quite religious, telling the story of the Nativity and ending with the essential message of Christmas—that of love and brotherhood. Were it not for the last verse, this carol might be more rightly grouped as a simple Nativity carol. But the mention of love and brotherhood is so rare among our favorite carols that it is singled out here as evidence that the Christmas message was important to carol writers hundreds of years ago and is not merely a late nineteenth- or mid-twentieth-century topic.

The work first appeared in print in the eighteenth century, in a collection called *The Roxburgh Ballads*. When it was republished in 1827 it was described as "an ancient version sung in the streets of London." As such, it is most likely to have originally been a London street song, sung by *waits*, who were hired by the city of London to serve as watchmen. They were also licensed to sing out the hours of day or night, serenade visiting dignitaries, perform at weddings of the upper classes, and sing traditional songs during holiday seasons, including the Christmas season. In return they might receive food or drink or coin.

In Dickens's *A Christmas Carol* it is the happy sound of "God Rest Ye Merry Gentlemen" that so infuriates Scrooge that he threatens the caroler—possible a wait—to drive him away.

God Rest You Merry, Gentlemen

Traditional

Brightly

God rest you merry, gen-tle-men, Let noth-ing you dis-may, Re-

mem-ber Christ our Sav - iour was born on Christ-mas day; To

save us all from Sa - tan's pow'r, When we were gone a - stray. O____

ti - dings of com - fort and joy, Com-fort and joy, O____

ti - dings of com - fort and joy.

It Came upon
the Midnight Clear

This is the only popular carol whose words are more concerned with the message of Christmas than with the event of Christ's birth. The emphasis reflects Edmund H. Sears's background as a Unitarian minister. Unitarianism is primarily concerned with the effect of the message on how we live our lives today, rather than what has occurred in the past.

The emphasis on the message also reflects where and when it was written. In Boston in 1849, schools remained open on Christmas Day and everyone was required to attend. Workplaces remained open and absences were not excused. Boston remained under the spiritual influence of its Puritan founders, who regarded the celebration of Christmas as a pagan ritual more connected with homage to St. Nicholas than worship of God. Christmas was not a time of celebration in mid-nineteenth-century New England.

Sears set down his words with the fervent hope that the suffering of mankind could be relieved. Sears's intent, to send a message reflecting Unitarian concerns about the relief of abhorrent social conditions, is most clearly evident in the rarely heard third and fourth verses.

Sears's poem was published in a church magazine. Richard Storrs Willis, an editor and critic for the *New York Tribune* and a friend and pupil of Felix Mendelssohn, wrote the music. Whether he composed a melody specifically for the poem or whether someone else adapted a piece of music he had written is not entirely clear. Words and music were first published together in 1850.

This is the only popular carol written by a Unitarian and, significantly, it is the only carol that focuses on the message from the angels and hardly mentions the Nativity or Christ as the Redeemer or Savior.

It Came upon the Midnight Clear

Words by EDMOND H. SEARS
Music by RICHARD S. WILLIS

Moderately

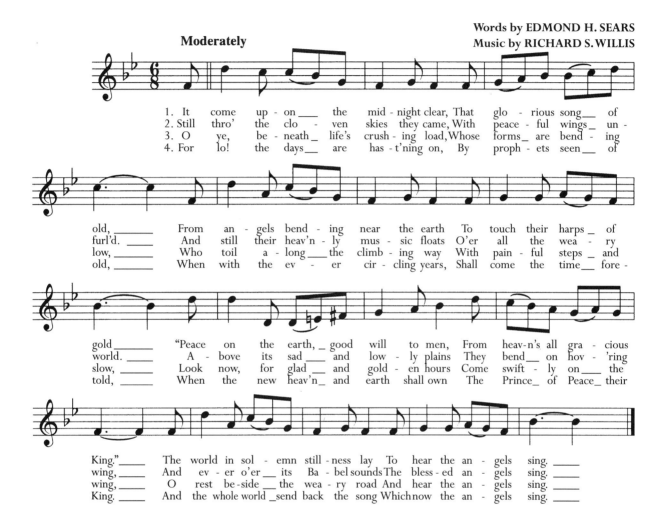

1. It come up-on ____ the mid-night clear, That glo-rious song___ of
2. Still thro' the clo-ven skies they came, With peace-ful wings_ un-
3. O ye, be-neath_ life's crush-ing load, Whose forms_ are bend-ing
4. For lo! the days___ are has-t'ning on, By proph-ets seen___ of

old, _____ From an-gels bend-ing near the earth To touch their harps _ of
furl'd. ____ And still their heav'n-ly mus-sic floats O'er all the wea-ry
low, _____ Who toil a-long ___ the climb-ing way With pain-ful steps _ and
old, _____ When with the ev-er cir-cling years, Shall come the time__ fore-

gold _____ "Peace on the earth, _ good will to men, From heav'n's all gra-cious
world. ____ A-bove its sad ___ and low-ly plains They bend__ on hov-'ring
slow, _____ Look now, for glad __ and gold-en hours Come swift-ly on ___ the
told, _____ When the new heav'n_ and earth shall own The Prince_ of Peace_ their

King." _____ The world in sol-emn still-ness lay To hear the an-gels sing. ____
wing, _____ And ev-er o'er __ its Ba-bel sounds The bless-ed an-gels sing. ____
wing, _____ O rest be-side __ the wea-ry road And hear the an-gels sing. ____
King. _____ And the whole world _send back the song Which now the an-gels sing. ____

December Pagan Festivals

Caesar invaded the British Isles in 55 B.C. and Roman garrisons stayed for the next four hundred years. They left an indelible imprint on British customs and traditions. As most of our carols ultimately came from Britain, an understanding of Roman holidays in December sheds a great deal of light on our Christmas customs and the origins of many carols.

At the time of Caesar's invasion there were two major Roman holidays in December: Saturnalia and Kalends. Saturnalia was named for Saturn, god of the harvest. Originally it was celebrated on a single day, December 17, but as the years went on it stretched to three days and finally to seven days. Only the first day continued to have any religious importance. The other days were given over to revelry.

Italy, with its warm Mediterranean climate, had an extra-long growing season and could harvest quite late into the year. The December date reflected local growing customs; the autumnal sowing was finished, there was ample food from the recent harvest, and the thinning of the herds need not begin until December. The conditions were right for a party—and from all reports they had wonderful parties.

Saturnalia was the merriest festival of the Roman year. The Greek Lucian reports the following legislation for the Saturnalia period:

All business, be it public or private, is forbidden during the feast days, save such as tends to sport and solace and delight. Let none follow their avocation save cooks and bakers.

All men shall be equal, slave and free, rich and poor, one with another. Anger, resentment, threats, are contrary to law.

No discourse shall be either composed or delivered, except it be witty and lusty, conducing to mirth and jollity.

There were great torchlight street parties with dancing and singing. Crowds ate and drank to excess and their shouts and cries prevented most Romans from getting much sleep. The traditional legal ban on gambling was suspended for the festival period. Homes were decorated with green boughs, and candles were to be seen everywhere.

The world was supposed to be topsy-turvy, and indeed it was. Masters waited on slaves at table and men dressed as women and paraded through the streets.

Every man shall take place as chance may direct; dignities and birth and wealth shall give no precedence.

All shall be served with the same wine . . . Every man's portion of meat shall be alike.

When the rich man shall feast his slaves, let his friends serve with him.

In ancient Babylon at the end of each year, the king was supposed to be put to death to ensure a new regime to welcome the New Year. To avoid their own demise, kings often appointed a captured enemy slave or soldier to be king for the day—after which he was sacrificed. Roman troops, who conquered all of the East, may have come in contact with some remnant of this Babylonian festival and brought it home. In Rome it took a less extreme form. A ''king for the day'' was chosen by lot, usually from among the servant class. His orders had to be obeyed and at the end of the day, he was not sacrificed, but simply went back to his former position. Aware that they would again be servants in the morning, most ''kings'' were rather sparing in their demands.

On December 31, the Romans began a four-day New Year's festival called Kalends. Originally the Roman New Year, like so many other ancient peoples' New Year's dates, was set to coincide with some agricultural event. In Rome it coincided with spring planting on March 1. But over the years Roman civilization became urbanized and paid less attention to rituals of planting and harvest. Finally, in 153 B.C., the date was moved to January 1.

The proximity of Saturnalia and Kalends to one another—and their occurrence after the harvest and the autumnal planting, when there was less work to be done in the fields—finally caused the two holidays to merge into a long two-and-a-half-week spree from December 17 until January 4.

The merging of the two holidays made many features of them indistinguishable. The parties and parades, the dancing and singing, the drinking and eating continued unabated. A fourth-century Greek, Libanius, described Kalends:

> The festival of the Kalends is celebrated everywhere as far as the limits of the Roman Empire extend. Everywhere may be seen carousels and well-laden tables; luxurious abundance is found in the houses of the rich, but also in the houses of the poor better food than usual is put upon the table. The impulse to spend seizes everyone. . . . People are not only generous towards themselves, but also towards their fellow men. A stream of presents pours itself out on all sides. . . . The highroads and footpaths are covered with whole processions of laden men and beasts. . . . As the thousand flowers which burst forth everywhere are the adornment of spring, so are the thousand presents, poured out on all sides, the decoration of the Kalends feast. . . . The Kalends festival banishes all that is connected with toil, and allows men to give themselves up to undisturbed enjoyment. From the minds of young people it removes two kinds of dread; the dread of the schoolmaster and the dread of the stern pedagogue. The slave also it allows, so far as possible, to breathe the air of freedom. . . .

What distinguished Kalends most from Saturnalia was the belief that the New Year offered an unparalleled opportunity for omens and portends of the future.

Gifts were exchanged and the gift chosen was often a symbol of what the giver wished for the recipient in the New Year. A gift of figs or dates represented wishes for a year full of sweetness. Nuts and figs might be gilded to wish someone prosperity in the coming year. Before an excess of spending set in, gifts of green branches were commonly given to wish for a good harvest. Gifts were expected by tradesmen, teachers, nobles, and landlords. It seems that everyone gave gifts to everyone, initially as a sign of wishing them well, but later as a sign of esteem.

The gift giving was largely restricted to the first day of celebration. On January 2, no more presents were given and it was customary to stay at home playing dice. All classes of people played together on this special day. January 3 was often given over to racing, while the forth and last day brought a tailing off of activities.

These festivals continued well after the fall of Rome. A sixth-century Christian sermon condemns the continued excesses of the holiday:

> [T]he heathen, reversing the order of things, dress themselves up in indecent deformities. . . . These miserable men, and what is worse, some who have been baptized, put on counterfeit forms and monstrous faces, at which one should rather be ashamed and sad. . . . Some are clothed in the hides of cattle; others put on the heads of beasts, rejoicing and exulting that they have so transformed themselves into the shapes of animals that they no longer appear to be men . . . men are clothed in women's dresses . . . the majority of men on those days became slaves to gluttony and riotous living and raved in drunkenness and impious dancing.

Saturnalia and Kalends accompanied Caesar's legions to Britain. Mithraism came later. Adopted by Roman soldiers when garrisoned in the Levant, Mithraism spread rapidly through the military and was made the state religion in A.D. 274.

Mithraism had many of the same features as Christianity. The resemblance may be due to the fact that both religions originated in the same part of the world at about the same time. These similar ideas may have been shared by many religions of that time and place whose existence is unknown to us.

Mithraism included purification through baptism, sacramental meals, and observation of a Sabbath-like day on Sunday. Its myths focused on good verses evil and heaven and hell. It even preached the defeat of evil through personal morality.

Mithraism was the official state religion of the Roman Empire at a time when Christianity was just gaining a foothold. As such, it was seen as the main antagonist with which the Christian church had to deal. Mithra was the Sun God and he was born on December 25—the solstice day in the old Roman calendar. And so Jesus became the Son of God, the light of the world, the rising sun of a new life—and his birthday was assigned to December 25. The Vatican was built on the very hill that served as the central focus for Mithra's worship.

Mithraism may live on in our ancient inheritance, blended with the Norse, Celtic, and Welsh celebrations of light. But Mithraism could not last. It was an all-male religion. Women who sought solace moved on to Christianity.

People who lived in northern climes—the Norse, the Celts, and the ancient Brits—tended to celebrate their New Year much earlier than the Romans. The reason was that the harvest finished much earlier and the thinning of the herds had to be finished at a much earlier date. The food would spoil if they waited too long. The Celts celebrated on November 1, as did most Germanic tribes.

Celtic celebrations focused on the reborn sun. Great bonfires lit the countryside as Druid priests sought to appease their sun deities. Embers were taken from the fires to kindle individual hearths. By medieval times, a number of Roman practices could be found among the Celts. The "king for a day" had been transformed into the Lord of Misrule. For the festival period, laws were suspended and gambling was allowed. The Druids regarded the mistletoe as sacred because it—like the holly—bore berries in the coldest of winters. They too prized all evergreens as containing the mysterious life force they were trying to harness.

Among the Welsh, amidst other bonfire festivities, we find the legends of Mari Llwyd, who appears as a horse skeleton in the night. The skeleton of the horse's head was mounted on the shoulders of a man who could work the jaws to snap at spectators. Similar rites are found in eastern and central Europe. Are these remnants of the animal-skin festivities of Roman times, or are both descended from sacrificed rites performed with horses by the barbarian horse cults who invaded Europe and probed the boundaries of Roman rule?

And finally we come to the Norsemen. They attacked Britain for hundreds of years, beginning in the eighth century, and started many settlements on its northern shores. Their descendants live today among the Irish, the Scots, the Welsh, and the English. Prominent in their December celebrations was the Yule log. A great log, usually the root-gnarled portion of a fallen oak, would be dragged to the fire and set ablaze. It was to last for the twelve days of Yule celebrating. The number twelve is significant, and we find echoes of it in Twelfth Night and the Feast of the Epiphany. Halls were decorated (*decked*) with evergreens and it was a time of great feasting. And no feast would be complete without singing.

Essentially all of these feasts occurred when the harvest was done and the thinning of the herds had begun. Meats would not keep, and once the slaughter was done, the feasting had to begin. In the north, the feasts originally occurred in October and November. Over time there was great improvement in the cultivation of meadow grasses; the increased quality of the hay made it possible to feed the animals in their stalls far later in the year. The thinning came later and later in the year. Finally, the time when thinning might occur could be determined by religious or other celebratory times rather than by the closing of the pastures. Gradually, most of these late-in-the-year celebrations began to coalesce around the time of the winter solstice.

Britain had been invaded by Angles, Saxons, Celts, Vikings, and Romans. The people stirred all of these influences together into their own December brew, and when they emigrated they brought their celebrations and their songs to the United States.

SEASONAL CAROLS

Each year, from late June to December, the moments of sunlight grow fewer. The days grow colder. The weeks grow more harsh. Imagine what it felt like to people who had no electric lights and for whom candles might be too costly to use on ordinary occasions. Imagine what the roads and fields were like without moonlight. Even today, though we live in well-lit environments, as November yields to December, many people suffer minor depression associated with the lack of natural daylight. Something in the human spirit requires daylight and cannot prosper without the sun.

Is it any wonder that the ancients anxiously watched the sky, awaiting that special day when the precious moments of daylight began to increase? To the ancients it was as if the sun had won a battle with the powers of darkness.

The solar cycle dominated the lives of ancient peoples. And the moment of the winter solstice, the day when the sun began its journey back to warm the earth, became a time for rejoicing.

Echoes of that rejoicing are found in many older carols. They do not refer to Christmas itself, but rather to a season of rejoicing that existed for thousands of years before Christ's birth. When the church chose December 25 for the celebration of His birth, they did so seeking to transfer some of that happy spirit to His coming.

CAROLS

The Holly and the Ivy

Some carols clearly reveal their non-Christian beginnings—though they have long since been converted to more holy purposes. In "The Holly and the Ivy," the pagan underpinnings clearly show through the Christmas veneer.

The carol echoes the most ancient of religious practices. The earliest religions often dealt with supernatural beings who lived in and influenced the growth of vegetation so important to everyday life. Plants and trees were thought to be inhabited by fairies or, in the case of majestic oaks, by gods.

Ivy was prized for its extraordinary ability to climb and spread. Holly was a source of wonder because in the dead of winter the holly was not only green and full of life, but produced a red berry fruit as well. In one version that dates to the sixteenth century, this original wonder in nature is clear.

Folk legends about holly suggested that witches hated it and would flee from it. When boiled into a tea, it was said to induce dreams that would foretell the future. Single women tied sprigs of holly to their beds to ward off the devil.

In England holly was regarded as a good-luck charm for men, while ivy was thought to be a good-luck charm for women. In early versions of the carol the holly represents a man while the ivy represents a woman. The battle of the sexes is revealed in the following tale:

An English knight invited his tenants and their wives to Christmas dinner. The knight greeted them with a toast: "You men of the holly, whoever among you is master of your wife, let him stand and sing us a carol." After a wait that must have seemed eternal, one man arose and whispered a very short carol.

The knight turned to the women. "Ivy, it is now your turn. Whichever of you is master of your husband, let her now stand and serenade us with a carol." At which point they all began to sing at once. The cacophony grew louder and louder. The knight laughed and above the din proclaimed, "The ivy is the master!"

The church, realizing the futility of trying to stamp out the superstitions and folk tales that had existed for thousands of years, instead tried to substitute theological symbolism for folk imagery. The Christian version is clumsy, not only in its poor rhymes, but because it retains the title mentioning both plants, while the words totally ignore the ivy and dwell only on the symbolism of the holly. In church hands the prickly holly leaves became symbols of the crown of thorns that Jesus wore as He bent under the weight of the cross He carried to His place of crucifixion. The red berries were said to resemble the drops of blood He shed.

THE HOLLY AND THE IVY

Moderately

Traditional Old French

1. The hol - ly and __ the i - vy, Now both__ are full __ well grown, _____ Of all the trees that are in the wood, The hol - ly bears the crown. _____ O the ris - ing of the sun, The run - ning of __ the deer, _____ The play - ing of the mer-ry or-gan, Sweet sing - ing in__ the quire, _____ Sweet sing - ing in the quire. _____

2. The hol - ly bears _ a blos - som As white_ as lil - ly flow'r: _____ And Ma - ry bore sweet Je - sus Christ, To be our sweet Sav - ior. _____

Deck the Halls

The music of this carol is a traditional Welsh melody that may date back thousands of years. The words refer to ancient Celtic celebrations at wintertime.

The song refers to having a party. For parties the ancients decorated their temples—and sometimes their homes—with evergreens. The evergreen contained the essence of the mysterious life force. How did it remain green in the winter while other plants shriveled and died? How did holly bear bright red fruit in the snow? The evergreen was a symbol of the triumph of life over the withering death that winter brings. And so the Celts decorated with evergreens and holly to celebrate the return of the life-giving sun.

The word *Yuletide* refers to the old heathen festival that lasted twelve days after the winter solstice. The word *Yule* is from the ancient Celtic word *hail* or the related Nordic word *rol*, both meaning "wheel" and referring to the cycle of the sun. Happy that daylight will triumph over darkness, the revelers dress up to celebrate. The Yule log is dragged in and set ablaze. The music of the Celtic harp begins, and people begin to sing and dance.

There isn't a single mention of Christmas or the Nativity. In this carol we can glimpse the merrymaking and fun that ushered in the winter season before Christianity usurped the holiday for its own purposes.

DECK THE HALLS

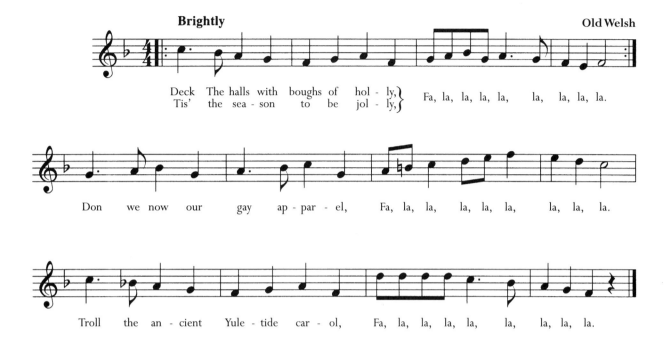

Brightly

Old Welsh

Deck The halls with boughs of hol - ly,}
Tis' the sea - son to be jol - ly,} Fa, la, la, la, la, la, la, la, la.

Don we now our gay ap - par - el, Fa, la, la, la, la, la, la, la, la.

Troll the an - cient Yule - tide car - ol, Fa, la, la, la, la, la, la, la, la.

Here We Come A-Wassailing

The Anglo-Saxon word *waes-heil* means "be well." It was used as a toast, much as we say "to your health." In its earliest form it was probably used to drink to the health of the lord of the manor. The proper response among Anglo-Saxons was *drine-heil*, or "drink well," much as we would say "down the hatch," as they ladled out a cup for the peasants.

The custom in medieval England was to celebrate the holiday season with a great punch bowl of heated brew. At that time the brew was called "lamb's wool" and was made with heated ale, eggs, cream, nuts, fruits, and spices. Later the recipes included imported spices and more potent, imported spirits, reflecting a growing affluence:

> Warm a mixture of cardamom, clove, nutmeg, mace, ginger, cinnamon, and coriander; port, sherry, or Madeira; and sugar. As it boils, whip in egg yolks and then, separately, whites of egg to make it froth. Add apples and serve hot.

The poor would go from door to door, cup in hand, begging a glass of punch. These visits were referred to as going "wassailing." Children also went from door to door, asking for sweets and coins. Among both adults and children the requests were often made in rhyme. Gradually the word *wassailing* came to be applied to the rhymes and, in later years, to the carols they sang.

Today, the most widely sung version is the children's version. The mention of "leaves so green" refers to the boughs of holly decorating the halls, and the one reference to Christmas seems forced and hardly rhymes. It may have originally referred to a Yuletide loaf. Clearly this is a seasonal song, intended to offer blessings for the new year in return for some food and coin. It is not Christmas, but the yearly cycle of the sun that is the cause for celebration.

HERE WE COME
A‑WASSAILING

Moderately

Old English

1. Here we come a - was - sail-ing A - mong the leaves so
2. We are not dai - ly beg - gars That beg from door to
3. Good mas - ter and mis - tress, As you sit by the
4. God bless the mas - ter of this house, Like - wise the mis - tress

green;_____ Here we come a - wan - d'ring, So fair _____ to be seen.
door; _____ But we are neigh - bors chil - dren, Whom you have seen be - fore.
fire, _____ Pray think of us poor chil - dren, Who wan - der in the mire.
too, _____ And all the lit - tle chil - dren, That round the ta - ble go.

Love and joy come to you, And to you your was - sail

too. And God bless you and send __ you a hap - py New

Year, And God send you a hap - py New ___ Year.

The Twelve Days
of Christmas

This is another seasonal party song. It describes a celebration in progress. The foods are listed: partridge, turtledoves, pheasants (the "five golden rings" refer to the ring-necked pheasants). The music of "drummers drumming" and "pipers piping" may be heard, and the people are having a good time: "lords a-leaping," "ladies dancing." A French version published in 1866 retains the party atmosphere, but with its own Gallic slant on party giving:

good stuffing without bones
2 breasts of veal
3 joints of beef
4 pig's trotters
5 legs of mutton
6 partridges with cabbage
7 spitted rabbits
8 plates of salad
9 dishes from the chapter house
10 full casks
11 beautiful full breasted maidens
12 musketeers with their swords

Though the song is first found published in London in 1780, these types of counting songs were widely known, and often pagan in origin. Uneducated people thought that chanting these numbers had magical significance, because they knew something about the numbers that we have forgotten—if the singer is given one gift the first day, three gifts the second day (two turtledoves and a partridge), six gifts the third day, and so on, the total number of gifts given over twelve days is 364, enough for the whole year—plus one day of rest—until the next gift-giving season arrives.

Though the song refers to twelve days of Christmas, we know that Yule also lasted twelve days, and the song may predate the celebration of Christmas. In any event, it is one more seasonal party song with no apparent Christian relevance.

THE TWELVE DAYS OF CHRISTMAS

Moderately

Old English

1. On the first day of Christ-mas, my true love gave to me, a par-tridge_in a pear tree. 2. On the

sec-ond day of Christ-mas, my true love gave to me, Two tur-tle doves and a par-tridge in a pear tree.

3. On the third day of Christ-mas, my true love gave to me, Three French hens,
4. On the fourth day of Christ-mas, my true love gave to me, Four mock-ing-birds

1.
Two tur-tle doves, and a par-tridge_ in a pear tree.

2.
Three French_ hens, Two tur-tle doves, and a

par-tridge_ in a pear tree. 5. On the fifth day of Christ-mas, my true love gave to me,

Refrain

Five gold-en rings; Four _ mock-ing birds, Three French hens,

To next Verse | Last time only

Two _ tur-tle doves, and a par-tridge_ in a pear tree. tree.

6th Verse *To Refrain* 7th Verse

6. On the _ sixth___ day of Christ-mas, my true love gave to me,
7. On the _ sev-enth day of Christ-mas, my true love gave to me,
8. On the _ eighth__ day of Christ-mas, my true love gave to me,
9. On the _ ninth __ day of Christ-mas, my true love gave to me,
10. On the _ tenth __ day of Christ-mas, my true love gave to me,
11. On the e-lev-enth day of Christ-mas, my true love gave to me,
12. On the _ twelfth__ day of Christ-mas, my true love gave to me,

Six geese a-lay-ing, Sev-en swans a swim-ming,

E -

To Refrain   Verses 8, 9, 10, 11, 12   *To Refrain*

Six geese a-lay-ing, 8. Eight__ maids a-milk-ing, Sev-en swans a swim-ming, Six geese a-lay-ing.
9. Nine __ la-dies wait-ing,
10. Ten ___ lords a-leap-ing,
11. lev-en pip-ers pip-ing,
12. Twelve_ drum-mers drum-ing.

*This measure to be repeated as often as necessary, so that text may be sung in inverse order, ending each time with "Eight maids a-milking".

O Christmas Tree

In most American homes the Christmas tree is the centerpiece of the holiday celebration. This tradition is strong in America because so much of our heritage is from England and Germany, where the tree prominently overlooks the celebrations. In France and many other countries the centerpiece is not the tree but the *crèche*, or nativity scene. Presents are placed next to it, rather than under the tree.

Decorated evergreen trees are mentioned by Virgil, writing about Rome before the birth of Christ. Trees for the Saturnalia festival were decorated with candles and with gifts. When the Goths invaded Rome they may have adopted these customs and brought them into Germany.

Tree worship was popular among Germanic tribes and the Celts. In fact, the church tried to prevent the use of trees during Christmas celebration because of the pagan associations.

The words are from a Westphalian folk song, ''O Tannenbaum;'' the melody, which may date from the Middle Ages, may once have been a Latin hymn. There are a number of other versions, but, for the most part, they all pay homage to the changeless green leaves—the same miraculous life force noted in the holly and other evergreens.

The Christmas tree came to America with German immigrants, but got a major promotional boost when Queen Victoria's husband Albert introduced the tradition to England. The original English Christmas trees were quite small and stood on tabletops. Big trees were too important to waste for decoration.

What is clear from the words is that this carol refers to the tree and not to Christmas. It is one more of the carols that revel in the fun of the season and have little religious meaning.

There has been at least one attempt to make this into a more religious carol:

Oh Christmas tree! Fair Christmas tree!

You tell the timeless story.

Oh Christmas tree! Fair Christmas tree!

You speak of Jesus' glory.

With gifts of love and songs of mirth,

With tidings of our Savior's birth,

Oh Christmas tree! Fair Christmas tree!

You tell the timeless story.

But this more religious version has not caught on.

O CHRISTMAS TREE

Moderately

German Folk Song

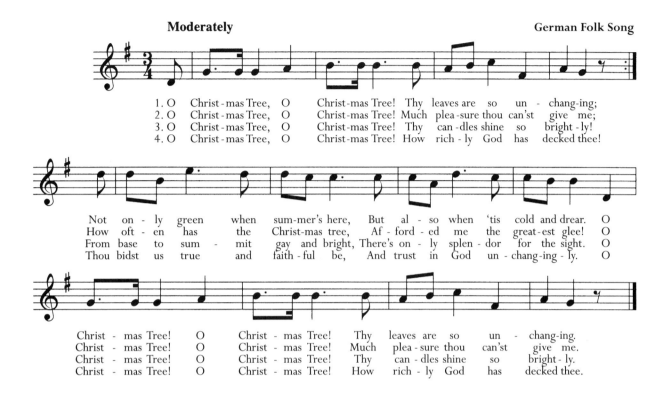

1. O Christ-mas Tree, O Christ-mas Tree! Thy leaves are so un - chang-ing;
2. O Christ-mas Tree, O Christ-mas Tree! Much plea-sure thou can'st give me;
3. O Christ-mas Tree, O Christ-mas Tree! Thy can-dles shine so bright-ly!
4. O Christ-mas Tree, O Christ-mas Tree! How rich-ly God has decked thee!

Not on - ly green when sum-mer's here, But al - so when 'tis cold and drear. O
How oft - en has the Christ-mas tree, Af - ford - ed me the great-est glee! O
From base to sum - mit gay and bright, There's on - ly splen - dor for the sight. O
Thou bidst us true and faith - ful be, And trust in God un - chang-ing - ly. O

Christ - mas Tree! O Christ - mas Tree! Thy leaves are so un - chang-ing.
Christ - mas Tree! O Christ - mas Tree! Much plea-sure thou can'st give me.
Christ - mas Tree! O Christ - mas Tree! Thy can-dles shine so bright- ly.
Christ - mas Tree! O Christ - mas Tree! How rich-ly God has decked thee.

Jingle Bells

One of the most widely sung Christmas carols, "Jingle Bells," was originally written for a Thanksgiving program to be given by Sunday school children at a church in Boston. No wonder it does not contain a single reference to Christmas!

If the second verse were sung more often, it would be quite obvious that the song had no specific holiday intent. It is simply a joyous ride in the country. Most writers believe that the "jingle bells" refers to the collars adorned with bells frequently worn by horses. The jingling would be measured and cadenced. But at least one writer believes that "Jingle Bells" is a command—an instruction to ring the bells as one rides along. If that is true, then one is making merry and making a lot of noise, having fun on this sleigh ride.

James Pierpont taught Sunday school and had written the carol in 1857 for his class. They sang it so happily at the Thanksgiving program that they were asked to repeat it for the Christmas program as well. From that day on, it was associated with the Christmas celebration. Pierpont published the song under the title "The One-Horse Open Sleigh," but the "jingle bells" are mentioned much more frequently in the refrain, and the song took on a more popular new name.

Jingle Bells

Allegro Traditional

1. We're dash-ing thro' the snow   In a one horse o-pen sleigh   and
2. A day or two a-go,   I thought I'd take a ride   and

o'er the fields we go   A laugh-ing all the way.   The bells on bob-tail ring   They're
soon Miss Fan-nie Bright   Was seat-ed by my side.   The horse was lean and lank   Mis -

mak-ing spir-its bright   What fun it is to ride and sing a sleigh-ing song to-night.
for-tune seem'd his lot   He got in-to a drift-ed bank and then we got up-sot.

Jin-gle bells, jin-gle bells, jin-gle all the way   Oh, what fun it is to ride in a

one horse o-pen sleigh. Jin-gle bells, jin-gle bells, jin-gle all the way

Oh, what fun it is to ride in a one horse o-pen sleigh.

The Stories
Behind
the Christmas
Tales

The Christmas that the English-speaking world celebrates today was largely created by three writers—Washington Irving, Clement Moore, and Charles Dickens. Before they wrote their Christmas tales and poems, Christmas in England and America, if it was celebrated at all, was very different from the present-day holiday. The essential ''Christmas spirit''—that generosity and kindness that makes the holiday so unique—wasn't a part of it. We owe our idea of the Christmas spirit to these three men.

Before these men wrote the stories that created our modern Christmas, in the English and American middle classes Christmas was the day the rents were paid—a day when accounts were settled. It was often a day when the government was in session, businesses were open, students were expected to be at school, and there was little attention paid to religious matters. In the lower classes, and more as a remnant of ancient harvest and end-of-year celebrations than anything specific to Christmas, the day might be given over to gambling, drinking, and squandering one's money.

On the European continent it was very different. Europeans held Christmas celebrations with gift giving and a mixture of religious, familial, and communal warmth left over from earlier times. France, Germany, Italy and other European countries each had their supernatural gift giver—*Père Noel, Pelznickel,* and *La Befana*—but often, these were figures who came to judge whether you were deserving, rather than Moore's "fat, jolly old elf" who came down the chimney to drop off some gifts. European gift givers were often accompanied by a threatening, gnarled, little black figure—Black Peter or Knecht Ruprecht, who might hand out punishments instead of presents. Depending on your ethnic background, when you were a child, you may have been told that you might find coal in your stocking or get no gifts at all, if you weren't better behaved.

Once, English Christmas celebrations had been lavish. In the seventeenth century, Christmas revelries included elaborate plays and pageants. In 1633 the Inns of Court presented an evening's entertainment at a cost of twenty thousand pounds. But less than fifteen years later, after Oliver Cromwell had successfully deposed the king and assumed power in the name of Parliament, all Christmas celebrations were outlawed. No plays, no feasts, and no Christmas in England.

Cromwell's Puritans outlawed everything that was reminiscent of papal authority or was not specifically mentioned in the Bible—including the saints' days, the date of Jesus' birthday, and even mince pies. They kept the Sabbath and ignored most other holidays.

Other Protestant groups, such as the Quakers, Congregationalists, Baptists, and Presbyterians, agreed with his anti-Christmas philosophy, but preferred to support the monarch or had other differences with Cromwell. Cromwell was a cruel foe and zealous at rooting out his enemies. The other sects fled England to settle in America. The Puritans, Quakers, and Presbyterians brought their anti-Christmas sentiment with them when they settled in New England, in the Maryland hill country, and in the coastal areas of the Carolinas and Georgia.

Some Church of England Anglicans, the Protestant group most involved with the English monarchy, also fled and were scattered throughout the colonies. They continued to celebrate Christmas in their own way. English Episcopalians settled in Virginia, where they also chose to honor the Christmas holiday. French Huguenots settled inland in Georgia and observed their Christmas quite merrily, as did Moravians, who settled in Pennsylvania as well as having scattered settlements through New York and New England.

Writing in 1797, a Pennsylvania Quaker, Elizabeth Dinker, divided Philadelphians into three groups: Quakers, who paid no attention to Christmas Day; types who were religious and prayed; and others who "spend it in riot and dissipation."

During colonial times, eighty percent of American settlers were of English, Northern Irish, or Scottish descent. The majority of them did not celebrate Christmas. Another ten percent were Germans who did celebrate the day. The remainder were a mixture of nationalities, some of whom (the Dutch, who are most important to our story) did hold some sort of celebration even though they were Protestants.

In a time when road travel was long and tedious and no other forms of communication existed, these groups went about their lives in their own regions, scarcely aware of and unaffected by what was going on elsewhere. Most were in settlements consisting almost wholly of sectarians of their own kind. They had no need to look beyond their borders. If there were neighbors who held different beliefs, there were also those of their own religion to offer support. If Christmas was observed, each group did it in their own way. Overall, there was no *one* way to celebrate Christmas on which all groups could agree.

December had always been a pagan holiday, and some form of celebration—even if it wasn't a religious one—often occurred at the time of year when the herds were thinned and the harvest was done. Thus, though they were not official Christmas celebrants, some Quakers and Presbyterians, noting the practices of the Swedes or Dutch living close by, are reported to have had an extra-special dinner or two somewhere close to December 25 or on New Year's Day—though they would never admit to observing the holiday per se.

By the time of the Revolutionary War, America had also attracted new settlers who had no interest in religious matters of any kind. Many of them brought their after-harvest folk festivals with them. For some, the Christmas season was meant to be awash with drink and food and merriment. It was a noisy holiday, when guns were fired and firecrackers set off. There was an old tale that noise drove the devil away, but whatever the reason, these rough pioneer men loved to make lots of noise. John Chapman, writing about the 1830s when he grew up in South Carolina, recalled the following:

> [T]he young men of Dutch Fork retained many of the wild, frolicksome habits that their forefathers brought with them from the Fatherland. Perhaps the wildest of these customs was to ramble throughout the night on Christmas Eve, in companies of a dozen persons, from house to house, firing heavily charged guns. Having thus aroused the family, they would enter the domicile with stamping and scramble to the blazing fire, greedily eating the praetzilles and schneckilies, imbibe, with many a rugged joke and ringing peal of laughter, heavy draughts of a compound liquor made of rum and sugar, butter and alspice stewed together, and then with many a screech and holler rush into the night to visit the next neighbor.

From his description it would appear that the participants might be German or Dutch. Nor were the English immune to this clamorous rite. As early as 1705, in Salem,

Massachusetts—Puritan territory!—some complained of the Anglican minority firing guns and celebrating noisily. The present-day English custom—lately appearing more frequently in America—of pulling ''Christmas crackers'' at the dinner table is an anemic descendant of this more robust tradition.

Samuel Beck, writing of his boyhood in Pennsylvania in the late 1700s, remembered more frightening Christmas celebrations:

> They were a set of the lowest blackguards, who, disguised in filthy clothes and ofttimes with masked faces, went from house to house in large companies . . . obtruding themselves everywhere, particularly into the rooms that were occupied by parties of ladies and gentlemen, (and) would demean themselves with great insolence.

One did not need guns and firecrackers to make noise. In more refined Philadelphia, where Quakers held sway, those who did celebrate the day had a tradition of blowing horns. In the 1820s, Philadelphia newspapers reported that the blare of the tin horns kept many awake on Christmas Eve. In other cities, ''target companies,'' paramilitary fraternal organizations, would march off to some suburban locale for a day of drinking and shooting. Toward nightfall they would stagger back into town midst shouts and roars. In more rural areas, Christmas Day turkey shoots were common. Old-time Christmas apparently made an awful noise.

And gift giving was rare. Traditionally it was a time when a landowner might give gifts to his household staff, his employees, or his slaves. Giving a gift implied a dominant role for the giver and a subservient one on the part of the receiver. No wonder it was rare for friends to exchange gifts or for gifts to be given to one's children or one's relatives—with the exception of German communities, where gifts for children had become a time-honored tradition.

Newspapers of the time often failed to mention Christmas—even on Christmas Day. It simply wasn't a widely celebrated holiday.

And that was the situation that greeted Americans as they made their way into the nineteenth century. The federal government did not set national holidays. It passed that responsibility on to the states, who often left it up to individual communities. If a community contained people of diverse backgrounds, it was difficult to obtain agreement as to how Christmas should be celebrated, and, in some cases, whether festivities should be held on December 6 (St. Nicholas Day), December 24 or 25, January 1, or January 6 (Twelfth Night). And so any celebration of Christmas was finally left up to the individual family.

Christmas as an official celebration was largely ignored by the ''better'' people—

the ones who regularly went to church and ran the government—except among Virginia Episcopalians, Catholics, and various sects. But a semblance of old-style December pagan celebrations remained alive among the ''folk''—especially those who weren't too religious. Much of what we think of today as essential to Christmas was missing. There were no displays of generosity toward friends and relatives. Santa Claus was rarely evoked as a symbol of the holiday. There was little feasting or public display. Homes were not decorated nor Christmas acknowledged, except among certain minority groups. There was little in the way of warm, comforting, family celebration.

Washington Irving

Washington Irving, America's first successful home-grown author, was born in New York City in 1783. He grew up as Christmas celebrations around him declined. He wrote whimsical stories and sketches and today is best known for ''*Rip Van Winkle*'' and ''*The Legend of Sleepy Hollow*.'' By the time he wrote about the Headless Horseman of Sleepy Hollow, Irving was already famous for his tales of Christmas past.

In 1809 Washington Irving wrote *Diedrich Knickerbocker's History of New York*, which poked mild fun at the old Dutch settlers of New Amsterdam:

> At this early period was instituted that pious ceremony, still religiously observed in all our ancient families of the right breed, of hanging up a stocking in the chimney on St. Nicholas eve; which stocking is always found in the morning miraculously filled, for the good St. Nicholas has ever been a great giver of gifts, particularly to children.

Irving goes on to describe St. Nicholas as a patron of the Dutch settlement on Manhattan. St. Nicholas reappears in the book a number of times, most resonantly in Oloffe Van Kortlandt's dream:

> [A]nd lo, the good St. Nicholas came riding over the tops of trees, in that selfsame wagon wherein he brings his yearly presents to children, and he descended. . . . [H]e lit his pipe by the fire, and sat himself down and smoked. . . . And when St. Nicholas had smoked his pipe, he twisted it in his hat-band, and laying his finger beside his nose, gave the astonished Van Kortlandt a very significant look, . . . he returned over the tree-tops and disappeared.

These are the words to which we are indebted for the Santa Claus who fills our stockings and our children's dreams. Irving was the original American source of all that is known about Santa Claus. His book helped revive St. Nicholas Day celebrations and inaugurated annual St. Nicholas Day dinners at the New-York Historical Society. New Yorkers took Santa to their hearts—and in a city full of commerce, soon to be full of immigrants, there were few barriers to a merry seasonal celebration.

It might never have come about, had Irving not created a fabulous hoax. On October 26, 1809, one might have read a notice in the New York *Evening Post* that one Diedrich Knickerbocker, "a small elderly gentleman . . . not entirely in his right mind," had gone missing. The notice asked concerned citizens to notify the newspaper if they had any information. In those days, such a notice was sure to draw attention and become a major topic of conversation. A newspaper was rarely more than four pages; mainly politics and shipping notices. A notice of that type would—and did—set the town talking. Eleven days later a letter printed in the paper informed readers that a gentleman who might fit the description had been seen traveling north of the city—more news to discuss over a stein at the tavern.

Another ten days brought still another notice in the newspaper, this time from Knickerbocker's landlord. He had entered his tenant's room and discovered a "curious kind of written book . . . in his own handwriting." As the rent had not been paid, he would have to dispose of the book to satisfy the debt. Good citizens speculated what the book might contain. Before speculation could die down, just twelve days later, the book was published and was an immediate bestseller. No book previously published in the United States had ever sold so well. As Irving's biographer, Johanna Johnston, said:

> [Nothing] compared to the instant triumph of . . . Diedrich Knickerbocker's *History of New York*. There had never been a book in America like this one. It was a humorous epic, a Homeric saga, an Elizabethan masque and bawdy joke, a melange that borrowed from everything that literate Americans had even read.

Washington Irving's promotional skills had created a publishing event! His letters to the newspaper had everyone talking. Though the practice of Christmas had fallen into disuse, St. Nicholas has long been an English favorite. It did not take much to bring him back to center stage. With hanging up one's stockings referred to as a practice among "families of the right breed," St. Nicholas and the celebration of his day were making their way back into fashion.

Irving's book may have been the bestseller of its day, but new fashions were not created overnight in the days when there were no radios, telephones, or other means of quick transmission. The book was read, loaned to a neighbor, and reread, and slowly new traditions were spread through the countryside.

But Irving wasn't finished. Ten years later, in 1819 and continuing on into 1820, Washington Irving published a series of "sketches" of an old-fashioned Christmas celebration in an English country manor house—Bracebridge Hall. He begins by describing a ride in a stagecoach out to the country:

> The coach was crowded, both inside and out, with passengers, who, by their talk, seemed principally bound to the mansions of relatives or friends, to eat the Christmas dinner. It was loaded also with hampers of game, and baskets and boxes of delicacies; and hares hung dangling their long ears about the coachman's box, presents from distant friends for the impending feast.
>
> Perhaps the impending holiday might have given a more than usual animation to the country, for it seemed to me as if everybody was in good looks and good spirits. Game, poultry, and other luxuries of the table, were in brisk circulation in the villages; the grocers', butchers', and fruiterers' shops were thronged with customers. The housewives were stirring briskly about, putting their dwellings in order, and the glossy branches of holly, with their bright red berries, began to appear at the windows.

Irving's protagonist, one "Geoffrey Crayon, Gent," arrived at the hall and describes Christmas Eve in the second of five sketches that were published. His friend has invited him to his father's home and goes on to say:

> My father, you must know, is a bigoted devotee of the old school and prides himself on keeping up something of old English hospitality. . . . He is a strenuous advocate for the revival of the old rural games and holiday observances. . . . Being representative of the oldest family in the neighborhood, and a great part of the peasantry being his tenants, he is much looked up to, and, in general, is known simply by the appellation of "The Squire."
>
> My father was always scrupulous in exacting our holidays, and having us around him on family festivals. He used to direct and superintend our games with the strictness that some parents do the studies of their children. He was very particular that we should play the old English games according to their original form; and consulted old books for precedence and authority for every "merry disport." Yet I assure you there never was pedantry so delightful. It was the policy of the good old gentleman to make his children

feel that home was the happiest place in the world, and I value this delicious home feeling as one of the choicest gifts a parent could bestow.

Irving is telling us that he will give us a glimpse of Christmases that are no more—celebrations that reflect warm, sentimental family values, yet are full of fun and joy.

As we approached the house, we heard the sound of music, and now and then a burst of laughter from one end of the building. This . . . must proceed from the servants' hall, where a great deal of revelry was permitted, and even encouraged by the Squire, throughout the twelve days of Christmas, provided everything was done conformably to ancient usage. Here we kept up the old games of hoodman blind, shoe the wild mare, bob-apple, and snap dragon; the Yule log, and the Christmas candle, were regularly burned, and the mistletoe, with its white berries, hung up, to the imminent peril of all the pretty housemaids.

[T]he Squire . . . ushered us at once (into) a large old fashioned hall. . . . where there were the usual proportion of old uncles and aunts, comfortable married dames, superannuated spinsters, blooming country cousins, half-fledged striplings, and bright-eyed boarding school hoydens. They were variously occupied: some at a round game of cards; others conversing round the fireplace; at one end of the hall was a group of the young folks, some nearly grown up, others of a more tender and budding age, fully engrossed by a merry game; and a profusion of wooden horses, penny trumpets, and tattered dolls about the floor, showed traces of a troop of little fairy beings, who, having frolicked through a happy day, had been carried off to slumber through a peaceful night.

Describing the Squire, Irving gets to the heart of his purpose:

There is an emanation from the heart in genuine hospitality which cannot be described, but is immediately felt, and puts the stranger at once at his ease. I had not been seated many minutes by the comfortable hearth of the worthy old cavalier, before I found myself as much at home as if I had been one of the family.

(There) were several family portraits decorated with holly and ivy. Besides the accustomed lights, two great wax tapers, called Christmas candles, wreathed with greens, were placed on a highly polished buffet.

. . . [N]o sooner was supper removed, and spiced wines and other beverages peculiar to the season introduced, than Master Simon was called on for a good old Christmas song.

> *Now Christmas come,*
>
> *Let us beat the drum,*
>
> *And call all our neighbors together,*
>
> *And when they appear,*
>
> *Let us make such a cheer,*
>
> *As will keep out the wind and the weather . . .*

The supper had disposed everyone to gaiety, and an old harper was summoned . . . The dance, like most dances after supper, was a merry one; some of the older folks joined in it. . . .

As I passed through the hall on my way to my chamber, the dying embers of the yule log still sent forth a dusky glow; and had it not been the season when ''no spirit dares stir abroad,'' I should have been half tempted to steal from my room at midnight, and peep whether the fairies might not be at their revels about the hearth.

I had scarcely got into bed when a strain of music seemed to break forth in the air just below the window. I listened and found it proceeded from a band, which I concluded to be the waits from some neighboring village. They went round the house, playing under the windows.

Geoffrey Crayon falls asleep, and when he wakes the next morning:

I heard the sound of little feet pattering outside of the door, and a whispering consultation. Presently a choir of small voices chanted forth an old Christmas carol, the burden of which was . . .

> *Rejoice our Saviour he was born*
>
> *On Christmas day in the morning*

I rose softly, slipped on my clothes, opened the door suddenly, and beheld one of the most beautiful fairy groups that a painter could imagine. It consisted of a boy and two girls. . . . They were going the rounds of the house, singing at every chamber door, but my sudden appearance frightened them into bashfulness.

Everything conspired to produce kind and happy feelings, in this stronghold of old-fashioned hospitality.

I had scarcely dressed myself when a servant appeared to invite me to family prayers. He showed me the way to a small chapel in the old wing of the house where I found the principal part of the family already assembled in a kind of gallery . . . and the servants were seated on benches below. The old gentleman read prayers from a desk in front of the gallery.

The service was followed by a Christmas carol which Mr. Bracebridge himself had constructed from a poem of his favorite author, Herrick . . .

> *'Tis thou that crown'st my glittering hearth with guiltless mirth,*
>
> *And giv'st me Wassaile bowles to drink spiced to the brink;*
>
> *Lord, 'tis thy plenty-dropping hand that soiles my land;*
>
> *And giv'st me for my bushell sowne, twice ten for one.*

I afterwards understood that early morning service was read on every Sunday and saint's day throughout the year. . . . It was once almost universally the case at the seats of the nobility and gentry of England, and is much to be regretted that the custom is falling into neglect.

Is this a carol of Christmas? It seems more like a song of thanksgiving for a bountiful harvest! The household moves on to attend services at the village church. Most of Irving's report on what happened at the church focuses on the orchestra and choir, but he does mention the sermon:

The parson gave us a most erudite sermon on the rites and ceremonies of Christmas, and the propriety of observing it, not merely as a day of thanksgiving, but of rejoicing; supporting the correctness of his opinions by the earliest usages of the church and the authorities of . . . a cloud more of saints and fathers from whom he made copious quotations.

There is little that is somber or penitent in this sermon, nor is there any report of the significance of Christ's birth. Whether this reflects what actually happened or whether it reflects selective reporting by Irving is difficult to ascertain. When Irving was a child, his father, William, had been a deacon in the Scottish Presbyterian church and is described as a somber, dour man. He taught his son that everything pleasurable was wicked. Irving had long since rebelled against church teachings, and the description he included may have sought to steep clear of religious preaching altogether.

After church they made their way, on foot, back to the hall. The villagers doffed their hats to the Squire as he passed, giving him the good wishes of the season with every appearance of heartfelt sincerity, and were invited by him to the hall, to take something to keep out the cold weather.

We had not been long home when the sound of music was heard from a distance. A band of country lads, without coats, their shirtsleeves fancifully tied with ribbons, their hats decorated with greens, and clubs in their hands, was seen advancing up the avenue, followed by a large number of villagers and peasantry. They stopped before the hall door, where the music struck up a peculiar air, and the lads performed a curious and intricate dance, advancing, retreating, and striking their clubs together, keeping exact time to the music; while one, whimsically crowned with a fox's skin, the tail of which flaunted down his back, kept capering round the skirts of the dance, and rattling a Christmas box with many antic gesticulations.

The Squire tells Irving that the dance dates to Roman times and is a direct descendant of their sword dances. Finally they all sit down to Christmas dinner.

The dinner was served in the great hall. . . . A blazing, crackling fire of logs had been heaped on to warm the spacious apartment. . . . Suddenly the butler entered the hall with some degree of bustle; he was attended by a servant on each side with a large wax light, and bore a silver dish, on which was an enormous pig's head, decorated with rosemary, with a lemon in its mouth, which was placed with great formality at the head of the table. . . . The harper struck up a flourish (followed by) an old carol. . . . The table was literally loaded with good cheer, and presented an epitome of country abundance. . . . The butler brought in a huge silver vessel . . . the Wassail Bowl. . . . The old gentleman . . . raised it to his lips, with a hearty wish of merry Christmas to all present, he sent it brimming round the board, for everyone to follow his example, according to the primitive style; pronouncing it ''the ancient fountain of good feeling, where all hearts met together.''

The dinnertime passed away in this flow of innocent hilarity, and, though the old hall may have resounded in its time with many a scene of broader rout and revel, yet I doubt whether it ever witnessed more honest and genuine enjoyment.

Like his *History of New York*, these sketches were widely praised. Irving wrote to a friend:

> I feel almost appalled by such success and fearful that it cannot be real—or that it is not fully merited, or that I shall not act up to the expectations that may be formed. . . . [N]ow that it is so extravagantly bepraised I begin to feel afraid that I shall not do as well again.

Why had this form of celebrating died away? In part it had to do with Cromwellian reforms and the new practices that Protestantism brought. But Irving does not describe a religious holiday—nor a raucous one. Irving describes what had once been a common Christmas celebration when England's economic system was dominated by the country manor. As was true of serfs in medieval Europe, in the manor system, farmers were tied to the land in various ways. The manor and its tenants formed a mutually dependent community, but offered little in the way of advancement. The dawning of a new commercial age was attracting families to the cities. Trade and travel had expanded, and many moved from the country manor to greater opportunity and a new way of life. Irving's account was a plea for a return to at least one aspect of the manor system— the paternalism that squires felt for their farmers, which was expressed most lavishly on Christmas Day.

Washington Irving painted warm and merry scenes in these Christmas sketches. Many of the same elements may be found in our present-day celebrations. But from a modern perspective, note what is missing. There is no ritual of gift giving. There is no mention of Santa Claus, nor of the English Father Christmas. There is no Christmas tree. Apart from the ritual attendance at church on a feast day, there is little or no mention of the Christ child, no representation of the Nativity, no direct acknowledgment of the day's very special religious significance. Even the church sermon is devoted to enjoyment and thanks for abundance. In fact, what is described seems like it must be very similar to the practices of the old pagan harvest holiday, with the name "Christmas" merely tacked on. Nevertheless, Irving altered a nation's habits with his sketches. As his biographer, Philip McFarland, points out:

> [B]efore the 1820s, in Puritan and post-Puritan America, the Christmas season had been only somberly and briefly observed. It was Irving who first enveloped the season for English-speaking readers with the warmth of blazing

fires on fine, clear frosty mornings, with the Christmas banquet of a boar's head decorated with lemon and rosemary, with the climactic Wassail Bowl made of the richest and raciest wines, highly spiced and sweetened, ''roasted apples bobbing upon the surface.'' He gives us scenes, in short, of good cheer and innocent hilarity that still may make old walls ring with merriment ''echoing back the joviality of long departed years.''

This is a secular, folk-tradition, Christmas celebration. It is the core of our modern public Christmas celebrations, as well as most private ones. Pagan holidays were celebrated in some similar fashion since long before the birth of Christ. Irving's skills brought it back into fashion and strongly influenced the other major tales that were to carry the message of a happy, generous, hospitable Christmas that brings joy to our hearts.

But there may be another reason why it was so readily adopted by Americans. America was growing prosperous. Over the next twenty-five years it would see the rise of a large, new, moneyed middle class. Like newly arrived middle-class people of our own time, they sought to legitimize their positions through imitating what were often referred to as their ''betters''—in this case, the old landed gentry. While our modern baby boomers have created a huge demand for antiques and certified paintings, the *arrivistes* in Irving's time created a huge market for piano manufacturers and fine cabinetmakers. Irving described for them how they might celebrate their Christmas ''properly,'' the way the gentry was supposed to have done—with benevolence and charity.

Clement Moore

Irving's influence may readily be seen in the most famous Christmas poem of all. In 1822 the Reverend Clement Moore, an acquaintance of Irving's, wrote ''A Visit from St. Nicholas,'' more popularly known as ''The Night before Christmas,'' for his children. Apparently he did not intend to publish it, and when it *was* published, it was years before he claimed any credit for it. Ironically, it was the only poem he wrote that has retained any degree of popularity.

Moore was from an old, established New York family of Dutch Walloon ancestry. The family home he inherited stood on a hill in lower Manhattan amid acres of farmland. In present-day terms, his holdings covered an expanse that was five blocks long and more than two blocks wide—over ten square blocks!

Moore was the son of the first Episcopal bishop of New York. Clement Moore donated the land upon which the Episcopal seminary was founded, and he became professor of Greek and biblical languages there. Apparently he had intended to become a minister, but changed his mind while attending Columbia University. He authored *A Compendious Lexicon of the Hebrew Language*, the first English-Hebrew lexicon printed in the United States.

Moore read the poem to his daughters Margaret and Charity, ages seven and six respectively, on Christmas Day 1822. A friend, Harriet Butler, was also there and copied the poem. Moore felt that his "children's poem" was a bit beneath the dignity of his position and did not wish to publish it. He feared it might damage his scholarly reputation as a lexicographer, poet, and professor. Harriet Butler was not to be put off and one year later, just before Christmas, she or a friend showed it to the editor of the *Troy Sentinel*, who published it as an anonymous poem in 1823, just a few years after Irving's Christmas sketches had been published.

The poem was an immediate success, and the *Sentinel* published it every year thereafter for many years. Other newspapers copied and printed it. One was the *New York Courier*, who by late 1828 had begun to query who had written it. The *Sentinel* editor, Orville Luther Holley, printed this reply on January 1, 1829:

> A few days since, the editors of the *New York Courier*, at the request of a lady, inserted some lines descriptive of one of the visits of that good old Dutch Saint, St. Nicholas, and at the same time applied to our Albany neighbors for information as to the author. That information, we apprehend, the Albany editors cannot give. The lines were *first* published in this paper. They came to us from a manuscript in possession of a lady of this city. We have been given to understand that the author of them belongs, by birth and residence, to the city of New York, and that he is a gentleman of *more* merit as a scholar and a writer than many of more noisy pretensions.

A "Dutch saint"? The attribution to the Dutch shows just how persuasive Irving's fiction had been. St. Nicholas was originally a bishop in Turkey. Legends of his kindness grew until he became the patron saint of Moscow and of Russia itself. Czars bore his name. "Nikita" means "little Nicholas." There used to be a saying among the Russians that "even if God dies, we still have St. Nicholas." By the thirteenth century, he had become the patron saint of children in Europe. In England, there are more than twice as many churches dedicated to him than there are to England's own patron saint, St. George. It shows how much he had been forgotten in America and how effective Irving's portrayal had been.

After many other publications of his poem, Moore finally allowed it to be published over his own name in *The New York Book of Poetry* in 1837, but he remained somewhat embarrassed by it right up to his death in 1863. It is doubtful that he ever understood how significant a contribution he had made.

'Twas the night before Christmas, when all through the house
Not a creature was stirring, not even a mouse;
The stockings were hung by the chimney with care,
In hope that Saint Nicholas soon would be there;
The children were nestled all snug in their beds,
While visions of sugar plums danced in their heads;
And mamma in her kerchief and I in my cap
Had just settled our brains for a long winter's nap,
When out on the lawn there arose such a clatter,
I sprang from my bed to see what was the matter.

Away to the window I flew like a flash,
Tore open the shutters, and threw up the sash;
The moon on the breast of the new fallen snow,
Gave a lustre of midday to objects below;
When what to my wondering eyes should appear
But a miniature sleigh and eight tiny reindeer;
With a little old driver, so lively and quick
I knew in a moment, it must be St. Nick.

Was the colloquialism "St. Nick" Moore's invention? It certainly made the saint less lofty and removed. It almost made him a part of the family.

The reindeer were a strange mode of transportation. The year before publication of Moore's poem, a friend and neighbor of Moore's, William B. Gilley, published *The Children's Friend: Number III, A New-Year's Present to the Little Ones from Five to Twelve*. It is now thought to have been written by a Presbyterian minister, Arthur J. Stansbury. One of the illustrations depicted Santa, on Christmas Eve (and not St. Nicholas Day—December 6), seated on a sleigh full of baskets of gifts, with the word "Rewards" boldly crowning the sleigh back. The sleigh is pulled by a single reindeer and underneath is printed:

Old Santeclaus with much delight
His reindeer drives this frosty night

O'er chimney tops, and track of snow
To bring his yearly gifts to you.

The steady friend of virtuous youth,
The friend of duty and of truth,
Each Christmas Eve he joys to come
Where love and peace have made their home.

Through many houses he has been,
And various beds and stockings seen,
Some, white as snow, and neatly mended
Others, that seem'd for pigs intended.

When e'er I found good girls and boys,
That hated quarrels, strife and noise,
I left an apple, or a tart,
Or wooden gun, or painted cart.

To some I gave a pretty doll,
To some a peg-top, or a ball;
No crackers, cannons, squibs or rockets,
To blow their eyes up, or their pockets.

No drums to stun their mother's ear,
No swords to make their sisters fear;
But pretty books to store their mind
With knowledge of each various kind.

But where I find the children naughty,
In manners rude, in temper haughty,
Thankless to parents, liars, swearers,
Boxers, or cheats, or base tale bearers,

I left a long, black, birchen rod,

Such, as the dread command of God

Directs a parent's hand to use

When virtue's path his sons refuse.

Unlike Moore's poem, full of good cheer and a Santa who does not judge but merely leaves gifts, Stansbury's poem is didactic and threatening. Moore may have borrowed his reindeer, but he turned away from the sentiment. Of course this may have happened because the sentiment is directed to instruct unruly boys, and Moore had only daughters. Moore's Santa is benevolent, merry, and generous. Like Irving's patron saint of New York, Moore's Santa is a figure of fun and generosity and has no lessons to teach.

Irving's Santa Claus legend was growing and taking on some of the added mythology that we know today. Irving had him riding over the tops of trees, in that "selfsame wagon wherein he brings his yearly presents." Moore also has him coming over the treetops:

More rapid than eagles, his coursers they came,
And he whistled and shouted and called them by name;
"Now Dasher! now Dancer! now Prancer! now Vixen!
On, Comet! On, Cupid! on Donder and Blitzen!
To the top of the porch! To the top of the wall!
Now, dash away, dash away, dash away, all!"

As dry leaves that before the wild hurricane fly,
When they meet with an obstacle, mount to the sky,
So up to the housetop the coursers they flew,
With the sleigh full of toys and Saint Nicholas too.
And then in a twinkling, I heard on the roof
The prancing and pawing of each little hoof.
As I drew in my head and was turning around
Down the chimney Saint Nicholas came with a bound.

Following Irving's lead, Moore described Santa quite vividly:

He was dressed all in fur, from his head to his foot,
And his clothes were all tarnished with ashes and soot;

A bundle of toys he had flung on his back,

And he looked like a peddler just opening his pack.

His eyes—how they twinkled! His dimples how merry!

His cheeks were like roses, his nose like a cherry!

His droll little mouth was drawn up like a bow,

And the beard of his chin was as white as the snow,

The stump of a pipe he held tight in his teeth,

And the smoke it encircled his head like a wreath;

He had a broad face and a round little belly

That shook when he laughed like a bowl full of jelly.

He was chubby and plump, a right jolly old elf

And I laughed when I saw him, in spite of myself.

Was Santa an "elf" so that he could fit into the chimney? Or was this a carryover of much earlier European traditions that often described the gift giver as a dwarf or as having a dwarf helper?

Moore later claimed to have based his portrait of Santa Claus on an old Dutchman, Jan Duyckinck, who had been the caretaker of their house. He was described as "fat, . . . jolly, . . . bewhiskered . . . known for the old pipe he kept clenched in his teeth." This portly, jolly figure bore little resemblance to the ascetic, tall, angular St. Nicholas figure that had been depicted up to that time and who may often be found in craft fair carvings even to this day.

A wink of his eye and a twist of his head

Soon gave me to know I had nothing to dread.

He spoke not a word, but went straight to his work,

And filled all the stockings; then turned with a jerk,

And laying his finger aside of his nose,

And giving a nod, up the chimney he rose,

Almost the same gesture as reported by Irving in Van Kortlandt's dream!

He sprang to his sleigh, to his team gave a whistle

And away they all flew like the down of a thistle;

But I heard his exclaim, ere he drove out of sight,

"Happy Christmas to all, and to all a good night!"

The spread of Moore's poem through the first quarter of the nineteenth century coincided with the immigration of a large body of Germans to the eastern farm country of the United States. Unlike English Protestants, these German Lutherans had not abandoned their Christmas festivities. It was celebrated as a family holiday with special emphasis on the children. Moore's poem, written for his children, fit right in with German Christmas trees, handmade toys, decorations, and carol singing.

In the spirit of the generosity he celebrated, Moore never asked for or received any royalties for his poem. That fact probably increased the number of times it was published, first in newspapers and later in illustrated books.

Irving's humane vision was spreading, and Christmas was beginning to come into its own.

Charles Dickens

It is not certain whether Charles Dickens knew Clement Moore's poem by the time he wrote *A Christmas Carol*. In 1843 Moore's poem, though a runaway hit in the United States, was apparently not well known in England. But there is no question that Dickens knew and loved Irving's works. In 1841 Dickens wrote to Irving:

> There is no living writer, and there are few among the dead, whose approbation I should feel so proud to earn. And with everything you have written, upon my shelves and in my thoughts, and in my heart of hearts, I may honestly and truly say so. . . . I should like to travel with you, astride the last of the coaches, down to Bracebridge Hall.

Dickens embarked on a lecture tour of America in 1842, reading and acting out portions of his novels. During that tour, he and Irving became good friends. But Irving drew back from the association after Dickens published various works that were critical of the United States.

Even Dickens's early work revealed Irving's hold on his imagination. Six years before *A Christmas Carol*, Dickens published "Christmas at Dingley Dell" in *The Pickwick Papers*. The description of the Christmas activities owes much to Irving's earlier work. It begins with Mr. Pickwick under the mistletoe:

> It was a pleasant thing to see Mr. Pickwick in the centre of the group, now pulled this way, and then that, and first kissed on the chin, and then on the nose, and then on the spectacles; and to hear the peals of laughter that were

raised on every side but it was a still more pleasant thing to see Mr. Pickwick, blinded shortly afterwards with a silk handkerchief, falling up against the wall, and scrambling into corners, and going through all the mysteries of blind-man's buff, with the utmost relish for the game, until at least he caught one of the poor relations, and then had to evade the blindman himself, which he did with a nimbleness and agility that elicited the admiration and applause of all the beholders. The poor relations caught the people who they thought would like it, and when the game flagged, got caught themselves. When they were all tired of blind-man's buff, there was a great game at snapdragon, and when fingers enough were burned with that, and all the raisins were gone, they sat down by the huge fire of blazing logs to a substantial supper, and a mighty bowl of wassail, something smaller than an ordinary wash house copper, in which the hot apples were hissing and bubbling with a rich look, and a jolly sound, that were perfectly irresistible.

Dickens also echoes Irving's philosophical humanism, urging the holiday as a source of generosity and goodwill.

"Our invariable custom," replied Mr. Wardle. "Everybody sits down with us on Christmas eve, as you see them now—servants and all, and here we wait, until the clock strikes twelve, and beguile the time with forfeits and old stories."

Just as they were doing when Irving arrived at Bracebridge Hall.

Irving, according to his biographer, Johanna Johnston, had paid little attention to social conditions when he lived in America. But he was living in Liverpool, where he had gone to take care of a failing family business, when he wrote the Bracebridge Hall sketches. His personal problems may have sensitized him to the plight of others. It was at this time that he wrote to a friend:

You have no idea of the distress and misery that prevails in this country! . . . It is beyond the power of description. In America you have financial difficulties, the embarrassment of trade and the distress of merchants but here you have what is far worse, the distress of the poor—not merely mental sufferings—but the absolute miseries of nature, hunger, nakedness, wretchedness of all kinds that the laboring people in this country are liable to. In the best of times they do but subsist, but in adverse times they starve. How this country is to extricate itself from its present embarrassments . . . I cannot conceive.

Irving saw these pitiful souls each day as he wrote his Bracebridge Hall sketches. Though he was no social reformer, it may have been these sights that formed the subtext of his tale of generosity and paternalism.

In comparison, Dickens was at heart a social reformer. He abhorred the poverty of London. He believed that education was essential to lifting the lot of the poor, and especially of the young. His writings reveal that he believed that the young had an innocence in them that if nurtured, through kindness, generosity and education, would help the lad develop into a generous, hospitable, warm-hearted man. But if the boy was ill-treated, if his natural goodness was corrupted, he would become a twisted and evil figure in his adulthood.

In *A Christmas Carol,* the Ghost of Christmas Past escorts Scrooge to Fezziwig's warehouse, where he once worked. It is Christmas Eve and the Ghost wants Scrooge to see what he had been like when he was a young man. The moral is Dickens, but the party, as described, owes some small debt to Irving.

The Ghost stopped at a certain warehouse door, and asked Scrooge if he knew it.

''Know it!'' said Scrooge. ''Was I apprenticed here!''

They went in. At sight of an old gentleman in a Welch wig, sitting behind such a high desk, that if he had been two inches taller he must have knocked his head against the ceiling, Scrooge cried in great excitement:

''Why' it's old Fezziwig! Bless his heart; it's Fezziwig alive again!''

Old Fezziwig laid down his pen, and looked up at the clock, which pointed to the hour of seven. He rubbed his hands; adjusted his capacious waistcoat; laughed all over himself, from his shoes to his organ of benevolence; and called out in a comfortable, oily, rich, fat, jovial voice:

''Yo ho, there! Ebenezer! Dick!''

In those days businesses usually stayed open until nine. Fezziwig's closing as early as seven was intended to show his generosity. His "organ of benevolence" refers to the pseudoscience of phrenology, which claimed to link each of various portions of the skull to a specific trait. Essentially, Fezziwig laughed from his head to his toes—but by specifying his "organ of *benevolence*," Dickens reveals an important character trait and seeks to make his point of the importance of good-heartedness at Christmastime.

Scrooge's former self, now grown a young man, came briskly in, accompanied by his fellow-'prentice.

"Dick Wilkins, to be sure!" said Scrooge to the Ghost. "Bless me, yes. There he is. He was very much attached to me, was Dick. Poor Dick! Dear, dear!"

"Yo ho, my boys!" said Fezziwig. "No more work to-night. Christmas Eve, Dick. Christmas, Ebenezer! Let's have the shutters up," cried old Fezziwig, with a sharp clap of his hands, "before a man can say Jack Robinson!"

You wouldn't believe how those two fellows went at it! They charged into the street with the shutters—one, two, three—had 'em up in their places—four, five, six—barred 'em and pinned 'em—seven, eight, nine—and came back before you could have got to twelve, panting like race-horses.

"Hilli-ho!" cried old Fezziwig, skipping down from the high desk, with wonderful agility. "Clear away, my lads, and let's have lots of room here! Hilli-ho, Dick! Chirrup, Ebenezer!"

Clear away! There was nothing they wouldn't have cleared away, or couldn't have cleared away, with old Fezziwig looking on. It was done in a minute. Every movable was packed off, as if it were dismissed from public life for evermore; the floor was swept and watered, the lamps were trimmed, fuel was heaped upon the fire; and the warehouse was as snug, and warm, and dry, and bright a ball-room, as you would desire to see upon a winter's night.

In came a fiddler with a music-book, and went up to the lofty desk, and made an orchestra of it, and tuned like fifty stomachaches. In came Mrs. Fezziwig, one vast substantial smile. In came the three Miss Fezziwigs, beaming and lovable. In came the six young followers whose hearts they broke. In came all the young men and women employed in the business. In came the housemaid, with her cousin, the baker. In came the cook, with her brother's particular friend, the milkman. In came the boy from over the way, who was suspected of not having board enough from his master; trying to hide himself behind the girl from next door but one, who was proved to have had her ears pulled by her Mistress. In they all came, one after another; some shyly, some boldly, some gracefully, some awkwardly, some pushing, some pulling; in they all came, anyhow and everyhow. Away they all went, twenty couples at once, hands half round and back again the other way; down the middle and up again; round and round in various stages of affectionate grouping; old top couple always turning up in the wrong place; new top couple starting off again, as soon as they got there; all top couples at last, and not a bottom one to help them. When this result was brought about, old Fezziwig, clapping his hands to stop the dance, cried out, "Well done!" and the fiddler plunged his hot face into a pot of porter, especially provided for that purpose. But scorning rest upon his reappearance, he instantly began again, though there were no dancers yet, as if the other fiddler had been carried home, exhausted, on a shutter; and he were a bran-new man resolved to beat him out of sight, or perish.

There were more dances, and there were forfeits, and more dances, and there was cake, and there was negus, and there was a great piece of Cold Roast, and there was a great piece of Cold Boiled, and there were mince-pies, and plenty of beer.

Negus was a mulled port or sherry with sugar and lemon that featured an orange stuck with cloves that was dropped into it while it was boiling hot.

The mention of mince pies is significant. Cromwell's government, in its zealous drive to eliminate all symbolism of Christianity not specifically mentioned in the Bible, had actually specifically outlawed mince pies when they outlawed Christmas celebrations. There was a superstition that the ingredients of mince pie (raisins, currants, orange and lemon peel, citron, eggs, and so on) echoed the gifts that the Magi brought to the Christ child. The Protestants would have none of that, and they banned the dish. Dickens is reaching into folklore to subtly make his point that Christmas has humane significance that goes beyond religion.

But the great effect of the evening came after the Roast and Boiled, when the fiddler (an artful dog, mind! The sort of man who knew his business better than you or I could have told it him!) struck up "Sir Roger de Coverley."

This was a dance that when performed in America was more popularly known as a Virginia reel, where the couples are arranged in two lines facing one another and dance around each other and around each other couple, before pairing off.

Then old Fezziwig stood out to dance with Mrs. Fezziwig. Top couple too; with a good stiff piece of work cut out for them; three or four and twenty pair of partners, people who were not to be trifled with; people who *would* dance, and had no notion of walking.

But if they had been twice as many; ah, four times: old Fezziwig would have been a match for them, and so would Mrs. Fezziwig. As to *her*, she was worthy to be his partner in every sense of the term. If that's not high praise, tell me higher, and I'll use it. A positive light appeared to issue from Fezziwig's calves. They shone in every part of the dance like moons. You couldn't have predicted, at any given time, what would become of 'em next. And when old Fezziwig and Mrs. Fezziwig had gone all through the dance, advance and retire, hold hands with your partner, bow and curtsey; corkscrew; thread-the-needle, and back again to your place; Fezziwig ''cut''—cut so deftly, that he appeared to wink with his legs, and came upon his feet again without a stagger.

To ''cut'' is a dance step. The dancer leaps in the air, and while aloft, alternates his feet, first one then the other in front, before falling to the ground again.

When the clock struck eleven, this domestic ball broke up. Mr. and Mrs. Fezziwig took their stations, one on either side the door, and shaking hands with every person individually as he or she went out, wished him or her a Merry Christmas. When everybody had retired but the two 'prentices, they did the same to them; and thus the cheerful voices died away, and the lads were left to their beds; which were under a counter in the back-shop.

During the whole of this time, Scrooge had acted like a man out of his wits. His heart and soul were in the scene, and with his former self. He corroborated everything, remembered everything, enjoyed everything, and underwent the strangest agitation. It was not until now, when the bright faces of his former self and Dick were turned from them, that he remembered the Ghost, and became conscious that it was looking full upon him, while the light upon its head burnt very clear.

"A small matter," said the Ghost, "to make these silly folks so full of gratitude."

"Small!" echoed Scrooge.

The Spirit signed to him to listen to the two apprentices, who were pouring out their hearts in praise of Fezziwig: and when he had done so, said,

"Why! Is it not? He has spent but a few pounds of your mortal money: three or four, perhaps. Is that so much that he deserves this praise?"

"It isn't that," said Scrooge, heated by the remark, and speaking unconsciously like his former, not his latter, self. "It isn't that, Spirit. He has the power to render us happy or unhappy; to make our service light or burdensome; a pleasure or a toil. Say that his power lies in words or looks; in things so slight and insignificant that it is impossible to add and count 'em up: what then? The happiness he gives, is quite as great as if it cost a fortune."

The party is not unlike the one at Bracebridge Hall—though the circumstances are much reduced. There is food and drink, music, dancing, merriment, and joy. There is no religious quality to the celebration. There is no tree, no gift giving, no Santa Claus. It is simply a time to be warm-hearted and to spread what joy you can. It is one man's goodness toward his fellow human beings.

It was an age in which the Industrial Revolution was herding people into cramped, unhealthy living conditions. Wages were so low that even working families had to struggle to eat well. Dickens stressed the obligation that those who have should properly feel for those who have not. Dickens's Christmas was like Irving's Christmas, a time of good fellowship, goodwill to all, generosity, and kindness—but especially a lesson in noblesse oblige.

Those who were not kind or openhearted would, like Scrooge, suffer the torments of the damned. In *The Pickwick Papers,* six years before *A Christmas Carol* was published, Dickens made his point more concisely in a ghost story told to Mr. Pickwick by Mr. Wardle, the Squire at Dingley Dell.

THE STORY OF THE GOBLINS
WHO STOLE A SEXTON

"In an old abbey town, down in this part of the country, a long, long while ago—so long, that the story must be a true one, because our great grandfathers implicitly believed it—there officiated as sexton and grave-digger in the churchyard, one Gabriel Grub. It by no means follows that because a man is a sexton, and constantly surrounded by the emblems of mortality, therefore he should be a morose and melancholy man; your undertakers are the merriest fellows in the world; and I once had the honour of being on intimate terms with a mute, who in private life, and off duty, was as comical and jocose a little fellow as ever chirped out a devil-may-care song, without a hitch in his memory, or drained off the contents of a good stiff glass without stopping for breath. But, notwithstanding these precedents to the contrary, Gabriel Grub was an ill-conditioned, cross-grained, surly fellow—a morose and lonely man, who consorted with nobody but himself, and an old wicker bottle which fitted into his large deep waistcoat pocket—and who eyed each merry face, as it passed him by, with such a deep scowl of malice and ill-humour, as it was difficult to meet, without feeling something the worse for.

"A little before twilight, one Christmas Eve, Gabriel shouldered his spade, lighted his lantern, and betook himself towards the old churchyard; for he had got a grave to finish by next morning, and, feeling very low, he thought it might raise his spirits, perhaps, if he went on with his work at once. As he went his way, up the ancient street, he saw the cheerful light of the blazing fires gleam through the old casements, and heard the loud laugh and the cheerful shouts of those who were assembled around them; he marked the bustling preparations for next day's cheer, and smelt the numerous savoury odours consequent thereupon, as they steamed up from the kitchen windows in clouds. All this was gall and wormwood to the heart of Gabriel Grub; and when groups of children, bounded out of the houses, tripped across the road, and were met, before they could knock at the opposite door, by half a dozen curly-headed little rascals who crowded round them as they flocked up-stairs to spend the evening in their Christmas games, Gabriel smiled grimly, and clutched the handle of his spade with a firmer grasp, as he thought of measles, scarlet-fever, thrush, whooping-cough, and a good many other sources of consolation besides.

"In this happy frame of mind, Gabriel strode along: returning a short, sullen growl to the good-humoured greetings of such of his neighbours as now and then passed him: until he turned into the dark lane which led to the churchyard. Now, Gabriel had been looking forward to reaching the dark lane, because it was, generally speaking, a nice, gloomy, mournful place, into which the townspeople did not much care to go, except in broad day-light, and when the sun was shining; consequently, he was not a little indignant to hear a young urchin roaring out some jolly song about a merry Christmas, in this very sanctuary, which had been called Coffin Lane ever since the days of the old abbey, and the time of the shaven-headed monks. As Gabriel walked on, and the voice drew nearer, he found it proceeded from a small boy, who was hurrying along, to join one of the little parties in the old street, and who, partly to keep himself company, and partly to prepare himself for the occasion, was shouting out the song at the highest pitch of his lungs. So Gabriel waited until the boy came up, and then dodged him into a corner, and rapped him over the head with his lantern five or six times, to teach him to modulate his voice. And as the boy hurried away with his hand to his head, singing quite a different sort of tune, Gabriel Grub chuckled very heartily to himself, and entered the churchyard: locking the gate behind him.

"He took off his coat, put down his lantern, and getting into the unfinished grave, worked at it for an hour or so, with right good will. But the earth was hardened with the frost, and it was no very easy matter to break it up, and shovel it out; and although there was a moon, it was a very young one, and shed little light upon the grave, which was in the shadow of the church. At any other time, these obstacles would have made Gabriel Grub very moody and miserable, but he was so well pleased with having stopped the small boy's singing, that he took little heed of the scanty progress he had made, and looked down into the grave, when he had finished work for the night, with grim satisfaction: murmuring as he gathered up his things:

> Brave lodgings for one, brave lodgings for one,
> A few feet of cold earth, when life is done;
> A stone at the head, a stone at the feet,
> A rich, juicy meal for the worms to eat;
> Rank grass over head, and damp clay around,
> Brave lodgings for one, these, in holy ground!

" 'Ho! ho!' " laughed Gabriel Grub, as he sat himself down on a flat tombstone which was a favourite resting-place of his; and drew forth his wicker bottle. 'A coffin at Christmas! A Christmas Box. Ho! ho! ho!'

" 'Ho! ho! ho!' repeated a voice which sounded close behind him.

"Gabriel paused, in some alarm, in the act of raising the wicker bottle to his lips: and looked round. The bottom of the oldest grave about him, was not more still and quiet, than the churchyard in the pale moonlight. The cold hoar-frost glistened on the tombstones, and sparkled like rows of gems, among the stone carvings of the old church. The snow lay hard and crisp upon the ground; and spread over the thickly-strewn mounds of earth, so white and smooth a cover, that it seemed as if corpses lay there, hidden only by their winding sheets. Not the faintest rustle broke the profound tranquility of the solemn scene. Sound itself appeared to be frozen up, all was so cold and still.

" 'It was the echoes,' said Gabriel Grub, raising the bottle to his lips again.

" 'It was *not*,' said a deep voice.

"Gabriel started up, and stood rooted to the spot with astonishment and terror; for his eyes rested on a form that made his blood run cold.

"Seated on an upright tombstone, close to him, was a strange unearthly figure, whom Gabriel felt at once, was no being of this world. His long fantastic legs which might have reached the ground, were cocked up, and crossed after a quaint, fantastic fashion; his sinewy arms were bare; and his hands rested on his knees. On his short round body, he wore a close covering, ornamented with small slashes; a short cloak dangled at his back; the collar was cut into curious peaks, which served the goblin in lieu of ruff or neckerchief; and his shoes curled up at his toes into long points. On his head, he wore a broad-brimmed sugar-loaf hat, garnished with a single feather. The hat was covered with the white frost; and the goblin looked as if he had sat on the same tombstone very comfortably, for two or three hundred years. He was sitting perfectly still; his tongue was put out, as if in derision; and he was grinning at Gabriel Grub with such a grin as only a goblin could call up.

" 'It was *not* the echoes,' said the goblin.

"Gabriel Grub was paralysed, and could make no reply.

" 'What do you do here on Christmas Eve?' said the goblin sternly.

" 'I came to dig a grave, sir,' stammered Gabriel Grub.

" 'What man wanders among graves and churchyards on such a night as this?' cried the goblin.

" 'Gabriel Grub! Gabriel Grub!' screamed a wild chorus of voices that seemed to fill the churchyard. Gabriel looked fearfully round—nothing was to be seen.

" 'What have you got in that bottle?' said the goblin.

" 'Hollands, sir,' " replied the sexton, trembling more than ever; for he had bought it of the smugglers, and he thought that perhaps his questioner might be in the excise department of the goblins.

" 'Who drinks Hollands alone, and in a churchyard, on such a night as this?' said the goblin.

" 'Gabriel Grub! Gabriel Grub!' exclaimed the wild voices again.

"The goblin leered maliciously at the terrified sexton, and then raising his voice, exclaimed:

" 'And who, then, is our fair and lawful prize?'

"To this inquiry the invisible chorus replied, in a strain that sounded like the voices of many choristers singing to the mighty swell of the old church organ—a strain that seemed borne to the sexton's ears upon a wild wind, and to die away as it passed onward; but the burden of the reply was still the same, 'Gabriel Grub! Gabriel Grub!'

"The goblin grinned a broader grin than before, as he said, 'Well, Gabriel, what do you say to this?'

"The sexton gasped for breath.

" 'What do you think of this, Gabriel?' said the goblin, kicking up his feet in the air on either side of the tombstone, and looking at the turned-up points with as much complacency as if he had been contemplating the most fashionable pair of Wellingtons in all Bond Street.

" 'It's—it's—very curious, sir,' replied the sexton, half dead with fright; 'very curious, and very pretty, but I think I'll go back and finish my work, sir, if you please.'

" 'Work!' said the goblin, 'what work?'

" 'The grave, sir; making the grave,' stammered the sexton.

" 'Oh, the grave, eh?' said the goblin; 'who makes graves at a time when all other men are merry, and takes a pleasure in it?'

"Again the mysterious voices replied, 'Gabriel Grub! Gabriel Grub!'

" 'I'm afraid my friends want you, Gabriel,' said the goblin, thrusting his tongue further into his cheek than ever—and a most astonishing tongue it was—'I'm afraid my friends want you, Gabriel,' said the goblin.

" 'Under favour sir,' replied the horror-stricken sexton, 'I don't think they can, sir; they don't know me, sir; I don't think the gentlemen have ever seen me, sir.'

" 'Oh yes they have,' replied the goblin; 'we know the man with the sulky face and grim scowl, that came down the street tonight, throwing his evil looks at the children, and grasping his burying spade the tighter. We know the man who struck the boy in the envious malice of his heart, because the boy could be merry, and he could not. We know him, we know him.'

"Here, the goblin gave a loud shrill laugh, which the echoes returned twenty-fold: and throwing his legs up in the air, stood upon his head, or rather upon the very point of his sugar-loaf hat, on the narrow edge of the tomb-stone: whence he threw a somerset with extraordinary agility, right to the sexton's feet, at which he planted himself in the attitude in which tailors generally sit upon the shop-board.

" 'I-I am afraid I must leave you, sir,' said the sexton, making an effort to move.

" 'Leave us!' said the goblin, 'Gabriel Grub going to leave us. Ho! ho! ho!'

"As the goblin laughed, the sexton observed, for one instant, a brilliant illumination within the windows of the church, as if the whole building were lighted up;

it disappeared, the organ pealed forth a lively air, and whole troops of goblins, the very counterpart of the first one, poured into the church-yard, and began playing at leap-frog with the tomb-stones: never stopping for an instant to take breath, but ''overing'' the highest among them, one after the other, with the utmost marvellous dexterity. The first goblin was a most astonishing leaper, and none of the others could come near him; even in the extremity of his terror the sexton could not help observing, that while his friends were content to leap over the common-sized gravestones, the first one took the family vaults, iron railings and all, with as much ease as if they had been so many street posts.

"At last the game reached to a most exciting pitch; the organ played quicker and quicker; and the goblins leaped faster and faster: coiling themselves up, rolling head over heels upon the ground, and bounding over the tombstones like foot-balls. The sexton's brain whirled round with the rapidity of the motion he beheld, and his legs reeled beneath him, as the spirits flew before his eyes: when the goblin king, suddenly darting towards him, laid his hand upon his collar, and sank with him through the earth.

"When Gabriel Grub had had time to fetch his breath, which the rapidity of his descent had for the moment taken away, he found himself in what appeared to be a large cavern, surrounded on all sides by crowds of goblins, ugly and grim; in the centre of the room, on an elevated seat, was stationed his friend of the churchyard; and close beside him stood Gabriel Grub himself, without power of motion.

" 'Cold to-night,' said the king of the goblins, 'very cold. A glass of something warm, here!'

"At this command, half a dozen officious goblins, with a perpetual smile upon their faces, whom Gabriel Grub imagined to be courtiers, on that account, hastily dis-appeared, and presently returned with a goblet of liquid fire, which they presented to the king.

" 'Ah!' cried the goblin, whose cheeks and throat were transparent, as he tossed down the flame, 'This warms one, indeed! Bring a bumper of the same, for Mr. Grub.'

"It was in vain for the unfortunate sexton to protest that he was not in the habit of taking anything warm at night; one of the goblins held him while another poured the blazing liquid down his throat; the whole assembly screeched with laughter as he coughed and choked, and wiped away the tears which gushed plentifully from his eyes, after swallowing the burning draught.

" 'And now,' said the king, fantastically poking the taper corner of his sugar-loaf hat into the sexton's eye, and thereby occasioning him the most exquisite pain: 'And now, show the man of misery and gloom, a few of the pictures from our own great storehouse!'

"As the goblin said this, a thick cloud which obscured the remoter end of the cavern, rolled gradually away, and disclosed, apparently at a great distance, a small and scantily furnished, but neat and clean apartment. A crowd of little children were gathered round a bright fire, clinging to their mother's gown, and gambolling around her chair. The mother occasionally rose, and drew aside the window-curtain, as if to look for some expected object; a frugal meal was ready spread upon the table; and an elbow chair was placed near the fire. A knock was heard at the door: the mother opened it, and the children crowded round her, and clapped their hands for joy, as their father entered. He was wet and weary, and shook the snow from his garments, as the children crowded round him, and seizing his cloak, hat, stick, and gloves, with busy zeal, ran with them from the room. Then, as he sat down to his meal before the fire, the children climbed about his knee, and the mother sat by his side, and all seemed happiness and comfort.

"But a change came upon the view, almost imperceptibly. The scene was altered to a small bed-room, where the fairest and youngest child lay dying; the roses had fled from his cheek, and the light from his eye; and even as the sexton looked upon him with an interest he had never felt or known before, he died. His young brothers and sisters crowded round his little bed, and seized his tiny hand, so cold and heavy; but they shrunk back from its touch, and looked with awe on his infant face; for calm and tranquil as it was, and sleeping in rest and peace as the beautiful child seemed to be, they saw that he was dead, and they knew that he was an Angel looking down upon, and blessing them, from a bright and happy Heaven.

"Again the light cloud passed across the picture, and again the subject changed. The father and mother were old and helpless now, and the number of those about them was diminished more than half; but content and cheerfulness sat on every face, and beamed in every eye, as they crowded round the fireside, and told and listened to old stories of earlier and bygone days. Slowly and peacefully, the father sank into the grave, and, soon after, the sharer of all his cares and troubles followed him to a place of rest. The few, who yet survived them, knelt by their tomb, and watered the green turf which covered it, with their tears; then rose, and turned away: sadly and mournfully, but not with bitter cries, or despairing lamentations, for they knew that they should one day meet again; and once more they mixed with the busy world, and their content and cheerfulness were restored. The cloud settled upon the picture, and concealed it from the sexton's view.

" 'What do you think of *that?*' said the goblin, turning his large face towards Gabriel Grub.

"Gabriel murmured out something about its being very pretty, and looked some-what ashamed, as the goblin bent his fiery eyes upon him.

" '*You* a miserable man!' said the goblin, in a tone of excessive contempt. 'You!'

He appeared disposed to add more, but indignation choked his utterance, so he lifted up one of his very pliable legs, and flourishing it above his head a little, to insure his aim, administered a good sound kick to Gabriel Grub; immediately after which, all the goblins in waiting, crowded round the wretched sexton, and kicked him without mercy: according to the established and invariable custom of courtiers upon earth, who kick whom royalty kicks, and hug whom royalty hugs.

"'Show him some more!' said the king of the goblins.

"At these words, the cloud was dispelled, and a rich and beautiful landscape was disclosed to view—there is just such another, to this day, within half a mile of the old abbey town. The sun shone from out the clear blue sky, the water sparkled beneath his rays, and the trees looked greener, and the flowers more gay, beneath his cheering influence. The water rippled on, with a pleasant sound; the trees rustled in the light wind that murmured among their leaves; the birds sang upon the boughs; and the lark carolled on high, her welcome to the morning. Yes, it was morning: the bright, balmy morning of summer; the minutest leaf, the smallest blade of grass, was instinct with life. The ant crept forth to her daily toil, the butterfly fluttered and basked in the warm rays of the sun; myriads of insects spread their transparent wings, and revelled in their brief but happy existence. Man walked forth, elated with the scene; and all was brightness and splendour.

"'*You* a miserable man!' said the king of the goblins, in a more contemptuous tone than before. And again the king of the goblins gave his leg a flourish; again it descended on the shoulders of the sexton; and again the attendant goblins imitated the example of their chief.

"Many a time the cloud went and came, and many a lesson it taught to Gabriel Grub, who, although his shoulders smarted with pain from the frequent applications of the goblin's feet, looked on with an interest that nothing could diminish. He saw that men who worked hard, and earned their scanty bread with lives of labour, were cheerful and happy; and that to the most ignorant, the sweet face of nature was a never-failing source of cheerfulness and joy. He saw those who had been delicately nurtured, and tenderly brought up, cheerful under privations, and superior to suffering, that would have crushed many of a rougher grain, because they bore within their own bosoms the materials of happiness, contentment, and peace. He saw that women, the tenderest and most fragile of all God's creatures, were the oftenest superior to sorrow, adversity, and distress; and he saw that it was because they bore, in their own hearts, an inexhaustible well-spring of affection and devotion. Above all, he saw that men like himself, who snarled at the mirth and cheerfulness of others, were the foulest weeds on the fair surface of the earth; and setting all the good of the world against the evil, he came to the conclusion that it was a very decent and respectable sort of world after all. No sooner had he formed it, than the cloud which closed over the last picture, seemed to settle on his senses, and lull him to repose. One by one, the goblins faded from his sight; and as the last one disappeared, he sunk to sleep.

"The day had broken when Gabriel Grub awoke, and found himself lying, at full length on the flat grave-stone in the churchyard, with the wicker bottle lying empty by his side, and his coat, spade, and lantern, all well whitened by the last night's frost, scattered on the ground. The stone on which he had first seen the goblin seated, stood bolt upright before him, and the grave at which he had worked, the night before, was not far off. At first, he began to doubt the reality of his adventures, but the acute pain in his shoulders when he attempted to rise, assured him that the kicking of the goblins was certainly not ideal. He was staggered again, by observing no traces of footsteps in the snow on which the goblins had played at leap-frog with the grave-stones, but he speedily accounted for this circumstance when he remembered that, being spirits, they would leave no visible impression behind them. So, Gabriel Grub got on his feet as well as he could, for the pain in his back; and brushing the frost off his coat, put it on, and turned his face towards the town.

"But he was an altered man, and he could not bear the thought of returning to a place where his repentance would be scoffed at, and his reformation disbelieved. He hesitated for a few moments; and then turned away to wander where he might, and seek his bread elsewhere.

"The lantern, the spade, and the wicker bottle, were found, that day, in the churchyard. There were a great many speculations about the sexton's fate, at first, but it was speedily determined that he had been carried away by the goblins; and there were not wanting some very credible witnesses who had distinctly seen him whisked through the air on the back of a chestnut horse blind of one eye, with the hind-quarters of a lion, and the tail of a bear. At length all this was devoutly believed; and the new sexton used to exhibit to the curious, for a trifling emolument, a good-sized piece of the church weathercock which had been accidentally kicked off by the aforesaid horse in his aerial flight, and picked up by himself in the churchyard, a year or two afterwards.

"Unfortunately, these stories were somewhat disturbed by the unlooked-for re-appearance of Gabriel Grub himself, some ten years afterwards, a ragged, contented, rheumatic old man. He told his story to the clergyman, and also to the mayor; and in course of time it began to be received, as a matter of history, in which form it has continued down to this very day. The believers in the weathercock tale, having misplaced their confidence once, were not easily prevailed upon to part with it again, so they looked as wise as they could, shrugged their shoulders, touched their foreheads, and murmured something about Gabriel Grub having drunk all the Hollands, and then fallen asleep on the flat tombstone; and they affected to explain what he supposed he had witnessed in the goblin's cavern, by saying that he had seen the world, and grown wiser. But this opinion, which was by no means a popular one at any time, gradually died off; and be the matter how it may, as Gabriel Grub was afflicted with rheumatism to the end of his days, this story has at least one moral, if it teach no better one—and that is, that if a man turn sulky and drink by himself at Christmastime, he may make up his mind to be not a bit the better for it: let the spirits be never so good, or let them be even as many degrees beyond proof, as those which Gabriel Grub saw in the goblin's cavern.''

The similarities to *A Christmas Carol* are striking. The central figure is a grumpy old man who does not celebrate the holiday (a warning to the many who had not yet taken up the holiday?). He meets with supernatural figures, as if in a dream, who humble and frighten him until he repents and changes his ways.

But what is missing in the tale of the sexton is the sympathetic characters he preys upon and the moment of redemption when he makes their lives merry. Perhaps that is why the tale of the sexton never became as popular as *A Christmas Carol*:

Running to the window, he opened it, and put out his head. No fog, no mist; clear, bright, jovial, stirring, cold; cold, piping for the blood to dance to; Golden sunlight; Heavenly sky; sweet fresh air; merry bells. Oh, glorious. Glorious!

"What's to-day?" cried Scrooge, calling downward to a boy in Sunday clothes, who perhaps had loitered in to look about him. . . .

"To-day!" replied the boy. "Why, CHRISTMAS DAY."

"It's Christmas Day!" said Scrooge to himself. "I haven't missed it. . . . Hallo, my fine fellow!" . . . "Do you know the Poulterer's, in the next street but one, at the corner?" Scrooge inquired.

"I should hope I did," replied the lad.

"An intelligent boy!" said Scrooge. "A remarkable boy! Do you know whether they've sold the prize Turkey that was hanging up there? Not the little prize Turkey: the big one?"

"What, the one as big as me?" returned the boy.

"What a delightful boy!" said Scrooge. "It's a pleasure to talk to him. Yes, my buck!"

"It's hanging there now," replied the boy. . . .

"Go and buy it, and tell 'em to bring it here, that I may give them the direction where to take it. Come back with the man, and I'll give you a shilling. Come back with him in less than five minutes, and I'll give you half-a-crown!" . . .

"I'll send it to Bob Cratchit's!" whispered Scrooge, rubbing his hands, and splitting with a laugh. "He sha'n't know who sends it. It's twice the size of Tiny Tim. . . ."

Through Dickens's skill the reader can feel the jubilation and the excitement. The triumph of the Christmas spirit is everything. And forever after, Scrooge was to be known as a man "who knew how to keep Christmas well."

Irving's tale of Bracebridge Hall held up the example of the rich man who is beloved because he does so many generous things for the less fortunate. That was his essential message for Christmas: The rich have the means to make the Christmas spirit manifest and if they do, they are much admired. Dickens, on the other hand, wrote cautionary tales: If a man has the means to make another happy—whether it is financial means or merely the means of kindness and benevolence—he will be damned if he does not do so, especially on Christmas. Again, the spirit of Christmas is kept if we are kind to one another and share our good nature or our good fortune.

These were eloquent messages for the dawning of the Industrial Age, when so many were in need. Dickens was trying to find a means to help the unfortunate, and the model in his mind—as in Irving's—was the old manorial system, when the paternalistic haves took care of the have nots.

At the time that Dickens wrote, many American communities did not celebrate Christmas. The majority of these were in New England, where there were holdouts until almost the end of the century. Other communities began to celebrate in tentative ways. Governments were reluctant to sponsor official celebrations, either because of the traditional American separation of church and state or because there were so many diverse heritages in any one community that it was impossible to agree upon a form of celebration that would please them all.

But commerce led the way. Stores began to stay open, decorate their windows, and offer goods specifically for Christmas. By 1830 New York stores stayed open until midnight during the week before Christmas. Other cities followed. Gradually, stores found ways of decorating and ways to present their goods that met with fewer and fewer objections from the community. In that way, a consensus was born and a style of Christmas emerged that all could agree upon. Even today, hardly a Christmas season goes by without someone complaining that this Christmas display or that offends their beliefs. It is all part of the process of reaching a national consensus on the proper way to celebrate what has become a national holiday.

Irving and Dickens had promoted a philosophy based on a return to the obligations and privileges of a society based on the manor system. With that system slowly fading at the end of the eighteenth century, their message fit the times and made sense to their readers. By the dawn of the twentieth century, few could recall the manorial system. In America, it became what had been practiced on the southern cotton plantations. That gracious way of life had been wiped out by the Civil War. Any memories that remained of life at the plantation house were out of step with the new realities of the Industrial Age. But people need to be reminded of the true spirit of Christmas. How could that spirit be presented in a manner that would connect with the lives of people in the first years of the new century?

And so, more than sixty years after *A Christmas Carol,* the American writer O. Henry brought the message of the Christmas spirit up to date. It was no longer a matter of charity from the rich. By then, the rich gave merely as a matter of propriety. The feeling was gone from it. Carnegie had given his libraries; Rockefeller made his contributions. Philanthropy had become institutionalized and depersonalized. O. Henry sought to restore to the act of Christmas giving, the human dimension that it once enjoyed. He told a tale of giving that was personal—and more poignant.

THE GIFT OF THE MAGI

One dollar and eighty-seven cents. That was all. And sixty cents of it was in pennies. Pennies saved one and two at a time by bulldozing the grocer and the vegetable man and the butcher until one's cheeks burned with the silent imputation of parsimony that such close dealing implied. Three times Della counted it. One dollar and eighty-seven cents. And the next day would be Christmas.

There was clearly nothing to do but flop down on the shabby little couch and howl. So Della did it. Which instigates the moral reflection that life is made up of sobs, sniffles, and smiles, with sniffles predominating.

While the mistress of the home is gradually subsiding from the first stage to the second, take a look at the home. A furnished flat at $8 per week. It did not exactly beggar description, but it certainly had that word on the lookout for the mendicancy squad.

In the vestibule below was a letter-box into which no letter would go, and an electric button from which no mortal finger could coax a ring. Also appertaining thereunto was a card bearing the name "Mr. James Dillingham Young."

The "Dillingham" had been flung to the breeze during a former period of prosperity when its possessor was being paid $30 per week. Now, when the income was shrunk to $20, the letters of "Dillingham" looked blurred, as though they were thinking seriously of contracting to a modest and unassuming D. But whenever Mr. James Dillingham Young came home and reached his flat above he was called ''Jim'' and greatly hugged by Mrs. James Dillingham Young, already introduced to you as Della. Which is all very good.

Della finished her cry and attended to her cheeks with the powder rag. She stood by the window and looked out dully at a grey cat walking a grey fence in a grey backyard. To-morrow would be Christmas Day, and she had only $1.87 with which to buy Jim a present. She had been saving every penny she could for months, with this result. Twenty dollars a week doesn't go far. Expenses had been greater than she had calculated. They always are. Only $1.87 to buy a present for Jim. Her Jim. Many a happy hour she had spent planning for something nice for him. Something fine and rare and sterling— something just a little bit near to being worthy of the honour of being owned by Jim.

There was a pier-glass between the windows of the room. Perhaps you have seen a pier-glass in an $8 flat. A very thin and very agile person may, by observing his reflection in a rapid sequence of longitudinal strips, obtain a fairly accurate conception of his looks. Della, being slender, had mastered the art.

Suddenly she whirled from the window and stood before the glass. Her eyes were shining brilliantly, but her face had lost its colour within twenty seconds. Rapidly she pulled down her hair and let it fall to its full length.

Now, there were two possessions of the James Dillingham Youngs in which they both took a mighty pride. One was Jim's gold watch that had been his father's and grandfather's. The other was Della's hair. Had the Queen of Sheba lived in the flat across the airshaft, Della would have let her hair hang out the window some day to dry just to depreciate Her Majesty's jewels and gifts. Had King Solomon been the janitor, with all his treasures piled up in the basement, Jim would have pulled out his watch every time he passed, just to see him pluck at his beard from envy.

So now Della's beautiful hair fell about her, rippling and shining like a cascade of brown waters. It reached below her knee and made itself almost a garment for her. And then she did it up again nervously and quickly. Once she faltered for a minute and stood still while a tear or two splashed on the worn red carpet.

On went her old brown jacket; on went her old brown hat. With a whirl of skirts and with the brilliant sparkle still in her eyes, she fluttered out the door and down the stairs to the street.

Where she stopped the sign read: ''Mme. Sofronie. Hair Goods of All Kinds.'' One flight up Della ran, and collected herself, panting. Madame, large, too white, chilly, hardly looked the ''Sofronie.''

''Will you buy my hair?'' asked Della.

"I buy hair," said Madame. "Take yer hat off and let's have a sight at the looks of it."

Down rippled the brown cascade.

"Twenty dollars," said Madame, lifting the mass with a practised hand.

"Give it to me quick," said Della.

Oh, and the next two hours tripped by on rosy wings. Forget the hashed metaphor. She was ransacking the stores for Jim's present.

She found it at last. It surely had been made for Jim and no one else. There was no other like it in any of the stores, and she had turned all of them inside out. It was a platinum fob chain simple and chaste in design, properly proclaiming its value by substance alone and not by meretricious ornamentation—as all good things should do. It was even worthy of The Watch. As soon as she saw it she knew that it must be Jim's. It was like him. Quietness and value—the description applied to both. Twenty-one dollars they took from her for it, and she hurried home with the 87 cents. With that chain on his watch Jim might be properly anxious about the time in any company. Grand as the watch was, he sometimes looked at it on the sly on account of the old leather strap that he used in place of a chain.

When Della reached home her intoxication gave way a little to prudence and reason. She got out her curling irons and lighted the gas and went to work repairing the ravages made by generosity added to love. Which is always a tremendous task, dear friends—a mammoth task.

Within forty minutes her head was covered with tiny, close-lying curls that made her look wonderfully like a truant schoolboy. She looked at her reflection in the mirror long, carefully, and critically.

"If Jim doesn't kill me," she said to herself, "before he takes a second look at me, he'll say I look like a Coney Island chorus girl. But what could I do—oh! what could I do with a dollar and eighty-seven cents?"

At 7 o'clock the coffee was made and the frying-pan was on the back of the stove hot and ready to cook the chops.

Jim was never late. Della doubled the fob chain in her hand and sat on the corner of the table near the door that he always entered. Then she heard his step on the stair away down on the first flight, and she turned white for just a moment. She had a habit of saying little silent prayers about the simplest everyday things, and now she whispered: "Please God, make him think I am still pretty."

The door opened and Jim stepped in and closed it. He looked thin and very serious. Poor fellow, he was only twenty-two—and to be burdened with a family! He needed a new overcoat and he was without gloves.

Jim stopped inside the door, as immovable as a setter at the scent of quail. His eyes were fixed upon Della, and there was an expression in them that she could not read, and it terrified her. It was not anger, nor surprise, nor disapproval, nor horror, nor any of the sentiments that she had been prepared for. He simply stared at her fixedly with that peculiar expression on his face.

Della wriggled off the table and went for him.

"Jim, darling," she cried, "don't look at me that way. I had my hair cut off and sold it because I couldn't have lived through Christmas without giving you a present. It'll grow out again—you won't mind, will you? I just had to do it. My hair grows awfully fast. Say 'Merry Christmas!' Jim, and let's be happy. You don't know what a nice—what a beautiful, nice gift I've got for you."

"You've cut off your hair?" asked Jim, laboriously, as if he had not arrived at that patent fact yet even after the hardest mental labour.

"Cut it off and sold it," said Della. "Don't you like me just as well, anyhow? I'm me without my hair, ain't I?"

Jim looked about the room curiously.

"You say your hair is gone?" he said, with an air almost of idiocy.

"You needn't look for it," said Della. "It's sold, I tell you—sold and gone, too. It's Christmas Eve, boy. Be good to me, for it went for you. Maybe the hairs of my head were numbered," she went on with a sudden serious sweetness, "but nobody could ever count my love for you. Shall I put the chops on, Jim?"

Out of his trance Jim seemed quickly to wake. He enfolded his Della. For ten seconds let us regard with discreet scrutiny some inconsequential object in the other direction. Eight dollars a week or a million a year—what is the difference? A mathematician or a wit would give you the wrong answer. The magi brought valuable gifts, but that was not among them. This dark assertion will be illuminated later on.

Jim drew a package from his overcoat pocket and threw it upon the table.

"Don't make any mistake, Dell," he said, "about me. I don't think there's anything in the way of a haircut or a shave or a shampoo that could make me like my girl any less. But if you'll unwrap that package you may see why you had me going a while at first."

White fingers and nimble tore at the string and paper. And then an ecstatic scream of joy; and then, alas! a quick feminine change to hysterical tears and wails, necessitating the immediate employment of all the comforting powers of the lord of the flat.

For there lay The Combs—the set of combs, side and back, that Della had worshipped for long in a Broadway window. Beautiful combs, pure tortoise shell, with jeweled rims—just the shade to wear in the beautiful vanished hair. They were expensive combs, she knew, and her heart had simply craved and yearned over them without the least hope of possession. And now, they were hers, but the tresses that should have adorned the coveted adornments were gone.

But she hugged them to her bosom, and at length she was able to look up with dim eyes and a smile and say: "My hair grows so fast, Jim!"

And then Della leaped up like a little singed cat and cried, "Oh, oh!"

Jim had not yet seen his beautiful present. She held it out to him eagerly upon her open palm. The dull precious metal seemed to flash with a reflection of her bright and ardent spirit.

"Isn't it a dandy, Jim? I hunted all over town to find it. You'll have to look at the time a hundred times a day now. Give me your watch. I want to see how it looks on it."

Instead of obeying, Jim tumbled down on the couch and put his hands under the back of his head and smiled.

"Dell," said he, "let's put our Christmas presents away and keep 'em a while. 'They're too nice to use just at present. I sold the watch to get the money to buy your combs. And now suppose you put the chops on."

The magi, as you know, were wise men—wonderfully wise men who brought gifts to the Babe in the manager. They invented the art of giving Christmas presents. Being wise, their gifts were no doubt wise ones, possibly bearing the privilege of exchange in case of duplication. And here I have lamely related to you the uneventful chronicle of two foolish children in a flat who most unwisely sacrificed for each other the greatest treasures of their house. But in a last word to the wise of these days let it be said that of all who give gifts these two were the wisest. Of all who give and receive gifts, such as they are wisest. Everywhere they are wisest. They are the magi.

AFTERWORD

The late-December celebrations were originally rooted in a very human condition, a sense of exultation that the light of the sun would return once more. It was as if, someone "up there" was watching out for the human race. It was also the time of year when men and women could relax a bit and enjoy themselves. Their larders were full from thinning the herds and harvesting the grain. By this time, some of the grain had fermented into beer. To this, Christianity added the joy that a Savior had come and that He brought a message of peace and goodwill. And finally St. Francis reminded us of the joys of home and family and that Christ—as a baby—brought simple joy into the world.

No wonder Christmas has given rise to such a diverse and wonderful legacy of songs and stories. There are many moods to Christmas. It is solemn and reverent, it is happy and boisterous, and it is warm and homely. Once these moods warred with one another, but today we seem to have found room for all of those feelings and a variety of other moods as well.

The standard sourcebook of carols is *The Oxford Book of Carols*. Its editor believes that carols are a direct expression of everyday people in plain language.

Carol literature and music are rich in folk-poetry and remain fresh and buoyant even when the subject is a grave one. The carol, in fact, by forsaking the timeless contemplative melodies of the church, began the era of modern music. The typical carol gives voice to the common emotions of healthy people in language that can be understood and music that can be shared by all.

Carols were always modern, expressing the manner in which the ordinary man at his best understood the ideas of his age, and bringing traditional conservative religion up to date.

And so our newer Christmas songs may well be on their way to becoming carols. After all, some of our newer Christmas songs merely restate old themes, in a voice and style more in tune with a modern audience. For instance, ''Rudolph the Red-Nosed Reindeer'' captures the timeless story of how the visit of someone with magical powers (in this case Santa Claus) can redeem a person's life. The song recognizes that the lowly and ostracized (in this case Rudolph with a nose so shiny that others make fun of it) can become heroes in spite of—or because of—their ''affliction.'' It is morally inherent in many old Christmas tales, and reminiscent of the most ancient of mystical feelings, that someone ''up there'' is watching over you.

On the other hand, new situations arise and the old carols may not have the right sentiment to fit the situation. World War II caused many to be away from their families at Christmas. A new type of song was created; a kind of blues-carol. ''White Christmas'' and ''I'll Be Home for Christmas'' captured the poignant sense of loneliness and wishful thinking that had not been captured in popular older carols. Despite their bluesiness, they are hopeful and positive (if not exactly buoyant) and fit the *Oxford* definition of what a carol should be. In these times of widespread divorce and the pressures of travel, one may be away from home and family without the trauma of war. These songs fit the description of ''expressing . . . the ideas of his age'' and ''bringing . . . religion up to date'' to fit modern life.

''The Christmas Song'' written by Mel Torme and Robert Wells is about the longing for the secular trappings of Christmas. It becomes all the more relevant as our modern lives and modern homes have less room for ''an open fire'' and children become prematurely skeptical about Santa Claus.

All of these songs may be on their way to becoming the carols of the next generation. Whatever their mood—reverent or playful, merry, homey, or longing—Christmas carols express what is in our heart.

Please join with me and let us raise our voices in song.

BIBLIOGRAPHY

Ackroyd, Peter. *Dickens*. New York: HarperCollins, 1990.

Auld, William Muir. *Christmas Traditions*. New York: Macmillian, 1931.

Chalmers, Irena. *The Great American Christmas Almanac*. New York: Viking Studio Books, 1988.

Charlton, James and Barbara Gilson (eds). *A Christmas Treasury of Yuletide: New York Stories and Poems*. New York: Galahad Books, 1992.

Davis, Paul. *The Life and Times of Ebenezer Scrooge*. New Haven, CT: Yale University Press, 1990.

Dawson, W. F. *Christmas: Its Origin and Association*. London: Elliot Stock, 1902; republished by Detroit: Omnigraphics, 1990.

Dearmer, Percy and R. Williams, et al. *Oxford Book of Carols*. London: Oxford University Press, 1964.

Del Re, Gerard and Patrica. *Christmas Almanac*. Garden City, NY: Doubleday & Co., 1979.

Dickens, Charles. *A Christmas Carol*. New York: Oxford University Press.

Duncan, E. *The Story of the Carol*. New York: Charles Scribner's Sons, 1911.

Editors of Life. *The Life Book of Christmas*, vol. 1. New York: The Glory of Christmas—Time Inc., 1963.

Ehret, Walter and George K. Evans. *International Book of Christmas Carols*. Englewood Cliffs, NJ: Prentice Hall Inc., 1963.

Gardner, Martin. *The Annotated Night Before Chrsitmas*. New York: Summit Books, 1991.

Gallico, Paul. *The Story of Silent Night*. New York: Crown Publishing Group, 1967.

Gilbert, Davies. *Some Ancient Christmas Carols*. 1822.

Godden, Rumer. "The History of Christmas," in *Book of Christmas*, Pleasantville, NY: Reader's Digest Association, Inc., 1973.

Hearn, Michael Patrick. *The Annotated Christmas Carol*. New York: Clarkson Potter, 1976.

Hill, Richard. *Not So Far Away in a Manger, 41 Settings of an American Carol in Notes*. Music Library Association, December 1945.

Irving, Washington. *Christmas at Bracebridge Hall*. New York: David McKay Company Inc., 1962.

————. *Diedrich Knickerbocker's History of New York*. New York: Heritage Press, 1940.

————. *The Sketch Book*. New York: Heritage Press, 1939.

Johnston, Johanna. *The Heart That Would Not Hold—A Biography of Washington Irving*. New York: M. Evans & Co. Inc., 1971.

Joseph, Robert. *The Christmas Book*. New York: McAfee Books, 1978.

Langstaff, Nancy and John. *Christmas Revels Songbook*. Boston, MA: David R. Godine, 1985.

MacDonald, Margaret Read, ed. *Folklore of World Holidays*. Detroit: Gale Research, 1992.

McBrien, Richard, ed. *HarperCollins Encyclopedia of Catholicism*. San Francisco: Harper-Collins Publishers, 1989.

McFarland Philip. *Sojourners*. New York: Atheneum, 1979.

Mottinger, Alvina H. *Christmas Carols, Their Authors and Composers*. New York: G. Schirmer, 1948.

Myers, Robert J., with the editors of Hallmark Cards. *Celebrations: The Complete Book of American Holidays*. Garden City, NY: Doubleday & Co., 1972.

Nissenbaum, Stephen. *The Battle for Christmas*. New York, Alfred A. Knopf, 1996.

Restad, Penne L. *Christmas in America*. New York: Oxford University Press, 1995.

Robbins, Rossell Hope. *Early English Christmas Carols*. New York: Columbia University Press, 1961.

Sandys, W. *Christmas Carols, Ancient and Modern*. London: R. Beckley, 1833.

Sansom, William. *A Book of Christmas*. New York: McGraw-Hill, 1968.

Scheffel, Richard, ed. *Discovering America's Past*. Pleasantville, NY: Reader's Digest Association, Inc., 1993.

Shekerjian, Haig and Regina. *Book of Christmas Carols*. New York: Harper & Row, 1963.

Simon, William L., ed. *Reader's Digest Merry Christmas Songbook*. Pleasantville, NY: Reader's Digest Association, Inc., 1981.

Snyder, Phillip. *December 25th: The Joys of Christmas Past*. New York: Dodd, Mead & Company, 1985.

Stevens, Patrica Bunning. *Merry Christmas, A History of the Holiday*. New York: Macmillian, 1979.

Studwell, William. *Christmas Carol Reader*. Binghamton, NY: Harrington Park Press, 1995.

Weiser, Francis X. *Handbook of Christian Feasts and Customs*. New York: Harcourt, Brace & World, 1958.

Wernecke, Herbert H. *Christmas Songs and Their Stories*. Philadelphia: Westminster Press, 1957.

Woodward, G. R., ed. *Pia Cantiones*. London: Plainsong and Medieval Music Society, 1910.